Personal Skills for Effective Learning

Annie Greeff

The Resilience Series

Crown House Publishing Limited
www.crownhouse.co.uk
www.chpus.com

Published by

Crown House Publishing Ltd
Crown Buildings, Bancyfelin, Carmarthen, Wales, SA33 5ND, UK
www.crownhouse.co.uk

and

Crown House Publishing Company LLC
6 Trowbridge Drive, Suite 5, Bethel, CT 06801-2858, USA
www.CHPUS.com

British Library of Cataloguing-in-Publication Data
A catalogue entry for this book is available from the British Library.

International Standard Book Number 978-190442437-6

Library of Congress Control Number 2004111625

Project management: Janice Baiton Editorial Services, Cambridge
Cover design: Tom Fitton, Crown House Publishing
Text design: Paul Barrett Book Production, Cambridge
Typesetting: Jean Cussons, Diss, Norfolk
Illustrations: Les Evans
Printed and bound in the UK by Gomer Press, Llandysul

Contents

Foreword

The Resilience Series is designed to provide an interactive learning process through which teachers, parents and others are able to empower children with useful coping skills. It offers relevant theoretical background information, structured guidelines for facilitating the learning process, and practical exercises and worksheets covering various related topics. *The Resilience Series* book aims to address personal, interpersonal and social competencies affecting life balance and quality of life. It encourages children to understand, appreciate and manage themselves, to form positive, meaningful relationships with others and to contribute constructively to society. In short, it has been written to help children become more effective learners.

The Resilience Series are books on psychology not a remedial tool for fixing problem or at-risk children. They are an attempt to offer a pro-active approach to integrated whole-person development, helping children in general to process and respond to what happens to them in a productive manner. From that perspective it could also assist at-risk children in their recovery, adaptation and healing through positive attention, a nurturing environment and the guided development of coping skills.

Contents are aligned with the Primary Strategy and those aspects of PSHE (Personal, Social and Health Education) and Citizenship required by the National Curriculum at Key Stage 2. And, of course, becoming a more resilient learner will help children to do better in all subject areas.

Through the use of these resource books, teachers will be able to communicate and connect with children on a significant personal level and to fulfil the roles of mentors or life coaches. Such caring relationships will enhance and balance the test-driven approach required for most subjects in the school curriculum.

Resilience theory encourages the engagement of children in the decision-making process about the curriculum. The teacher and the children could have a general discussion on the contents of the curriculum for a specific subject. For example, the material in this volume covers parts of PSHE. The children could be engaged in the process of deciding in which sequence the topics should be covered. This will help them take ownership of their learning process. They will have the opportunity to express their opinions and learning needs to their teacher. They can also help decide what the governing rules during the learning session should be. Eventually they can form peer support groups in which they support each other with academic and emotional issues.

When teachers ask questions that encourage critical thinking and dialogue, they engage children in the learning process. This resource book contains various activity sheets within each unit that can be used according to the children's needs, thus encouraging discussions and participative decision-making between children and their teachers/caretakers.

Annie Greeff
January 2005

Annie Greeff started her career as a teacher, but also gained experience in various other fields. In 1996 she became a Training and Development Consultant and has since developed and presented extensive ranges of Emotional Intelligence and Resilience or Wellness training programmes, facilitated group processes and offered life coaching for executives in various corpoarte companies. www.anniegreeff.com

Using this book

The Resilience Series is designed to facilitate the mastery of the personal and social skills needed to be an effective learner.

Each of the two **volumes** contains an introduction and a series of units covering, in this volume, Personal Skills for Effective Learning, and in the companion volume Social Skills for Effective Learning. Each **unit** comprises a theoretical introduction or broad overview of the topic, followed by guidelines for the teacher and activity sheets for the children.

Guidelines include:

● *Learning points* to clarify the aim or main purpose of the activity.
● *Comments* to guide the process and supply practical advice or potential responses where applicable.
● *Tips* to support the teacher in the presentation of the contents.
● *Timing* to indicate the approximate duration of instructions, activities and conclusion.

Activity sheets are:

● designed to structure the experiential learning process.
● photocopiable for usage by the children.

At the end of each unit, the Action Plan:

● summarizes the learning related to the topic.
● revises main learning points.
● acts as a stimulus for changes in behaviour or the strengthening/support of existing good habits.

May you and the children you teach experience great satisfaction, personal growth and a sense of purpose through the use of this series. Enjoy the journey!

Acknowledgements

My sincere gratitude to:

Piet, my loving husband, for being a loyal, supportive and generous partner in life.

Christine, Pieter and Van Heerden, my amazing three children, for enriching my life.

Hester, my mother, who demonstrated true resilience by raising six children on her own according to strong principles and deep religious beliefs.

Hottie, my late father, for leaving behind the legacy of kindness, generosity and humour.

Dr Susan Wolmarans, Lilian Niemann and Dr Melodie de Jager, my associates and friends, for contributing to the development of the *Resilience* books.

My many clients who, over the years, trusted me to work with their most valuable resource – their employees.

Scores of workshop participants who have attended my courses. Based on their feedback and enthusiasm, I have been able to deepen my understanding and refine my work.

Bill Lucas for his constructive feedback and guidance during the process of turning a participant workbook into two comprehensive resource books.

Janice Baiton for editing and project managing the two volumes.

David Bowman and others at Crown House Publishing for believing in the potential of the material in the books and making my dream of publishing my work come true.

Introduction

Outline

Introduction

Fostering resilience

Resilience is a broad concept, which includes the characteristics you need as an individual, your connection with others, and the support given by the environment you live in. In fact, when people develop resiliency traits and strategies on different levels, these protective strategies act together to create a strong, healthy cohesive society. The aim is to create an understanding of the interconnectedness of individuals, groups and society as a whole and thereby stimulate a sense of social responsibility while also acknowledging that each person can make a difference.

You can find out more about what resilience means in Unit 1, page 10.

Resilient people seem to have protective/support factors in three dimensions:

- individual
- relationships
- organization and environment.

The ideal strategy for fostering resilience is to develop coping skills within the individual and to ensure that the person experiences connection with others within a supportive environment. When support factors within and outside the person act in synergy, they 'automatically' compensate for the areas in which the person experiences difficulty. It is encouraging to know that when a person functions within a protective environment, over time, positive qualities form a stronger bond than that of the adverse influences.

If extreme old age (over ninety) is the ultimate proof of resiliency, research findings based on work done by Thomas Perls and Margery Hutter Silver (1999) indicate that the following traits are typical of well-adjusted, happy individuals in extreme old age:

- adaptability
- assertiveness
- sense of humour
- charisma

- involvement
- service to others
- sense of purpose
- caring relatives
- religion.

Age accelerators seem to be:

- regrets and bitterness
- detachment
- stubbornness to accept help
- compulsiveness
- emotional stress
- obesity
- alcohol consumption
- depression
- smoking
- inactivity.

We may not have control over the duration of our lives, but it is clear that we have significant control over the quality our lives, and many of the protective strategies are learnable competencies.

Resilience and effective learning

Self-esteem and social skills influence our learning abilities as they determine how we form relationships with ourselves, with others and even with information! In short, they form the basis of how we look at life. If resilience is the ability to bounce back from adversity or hardship, to overcome the negative influences that block achievement, then resiliency competencies enable learners to achieve excellence and enjoyment.

Emotional development and developing resilient learners

For young people, major emotional challenges include peer pressure and the resultant need to fit in with a group. They have a need to be accepted and to function successfully within a group. To fulfil that need they have to develop personal and interpersonal skills. When you understand and appreciate the application of what you learn, because you realize that the learning addresses your personal needs, the learning process will be more enjoyable and effective.

There is a saying that some situations are 'windows of opportunity' in terms of learning. When the learner is not ready, even the most impressive learning material may not reach its target. The opposite should also be true. If learning situations address specific needs at the right time, one could expect better results.

Typical traits in the emotional development of children in late childhood (6–11 years) seem to be the following:

- There is a desire to be part of the group and play according to rules, with the child wanting to be 'in'.
- The child experiences periods of heightened emotionality and would rather express than control their feelings.
- They can name feelings more readily.
- They thrive on praise and acceptance and have to work harder to understand and manage feelings.

Although we have to acknowledge that people develop at their own pace, broad categories offer useful guidelines. Based on the generic assumptions about this life stage, *Resilience* places strong emphasis on group-work and refining emotional competencies.

Resilience and the National Curriculum

The Appendix on pages 189–193 contains details about how resilience aligns with the National Curriculum outcomes for PSHE (Personal, Social and Health Education) and Citizenship.

Teachers as facilitators

Facilitating a typical work session

Facilitation

Facilitation in this context means non-directive guidance of a learning process. It is different from normal teaching. The emphasis is on asking the right questions and providing the right activities to enable young people to see for themselves what the possible results of changing behaviour or expanding behaviour patterns could be. Facilitation is therefore different from teaching, preaching, testing, telling, directing, lecturing, mentoring, coaching, counselling and leading.

Experiential learning, role play and games

Experiential learning means literally learning from experiencing the activity and reflecting on what was learned. It is not about listening to the expert but rather about simulating real-life situations, role playing, and participating in games.

In conventional schooling, the main focus is on the development of the mind. In experiential learning, the body, mind, thoughts, feelings and actions are involved. Experiential learning is therefore whole-person learning.

Group work and sharing ideas

Group work is vital for active participation and sharing. Most exercises are designed for small group activities, with feedback to the larger (whole) group. Active group participation promotes the learning of new skills, new attitudes and new knowledge about individuals as well as group dynamics.

The principle that 'none of us is as smart as all of us' becomes particularly evident in group learning. While group learning stimulates the refinement of group skills as basic life skills, great care should be taken to balance democratic facilitation, experiential learning and reflection.

It should be made clear that sharing is never forced and respect for privacy is encouraged, especially when some people may experience difficulty and feel sensitive about issues.

Reflection

Reflective activities may include individual reflection or group discussions aimed at integrating the learning process into existing frames of knowledge. This is done by observing, recapturing and evaluating the experience in an atmosphere of mutual respect and support. Although the activity sheets in this book are designed to simplify this process, children should also be encouraged to keep personal journals for further reflection and lasting learning.

Format of a typical learning session

Breaking the ice

The aim is to familiarize the children with the topic or main theme of the unit. Activities could take the format of fun exercises, movement, dancing, role plays or reflection.

Connecting to the self

This can be any exercise that allows the children to connect to personal experiences and existing frames of reference or understanding of the issue. Self-assessments are useful for this purpose.

Sharing with others

Creating an opportunity to discuss personal viewpoints as discovered/affirmed in the 'Connecting to the self' exercise.

Taking part in activities

An activity enables the thorough exploration of the main theme. It should involve all participants in experiential learning, either in the format of individual exercises or in a group context.

Giving and receiving feedback

Group sharing and formulating summarized responses of individuals or groups enable the larger group to share viewpoints. This could also include brainstorming sessions.

Reflecting

This covers learning from experience, own and others' opinions, and integrating the information into existing personal frameworks. It is about the expression of personal opinions and feelings and the application of knowledge and insights.

Making notes

Throughout the work session, notes could be made and displayed on a board or on sheets of paper. These would be the comments made by the participants and should be in their own words. Notes could also include analysis, summaries or conclusions and learning points.

Evaluating

By asking children which activities worked and what they did not enjoy or view as useful, the teacher is able to improve or expand on certain aspects of the workshop. Encouraging young people to give feedback demonstrates mutual respect, invites participation and ownership, and develops communication skills through the clear, tactful expression of personal opinions.

Resilience

I am flexible and strong

Outline

Outcomes

On completion of this unit, children should have the knowledge, skills and attitudes to:

- describe in their own words what it means to be a resilient learner.

- identify highly resilient people through media coverage of such people, or by observing resilient people in real life.

- list attributes of resilient people.

- understand how being multi-skilled and developing multiple intelligences support resiliency.

- name attributes or competencies they would personally like to develop.

- acknowledge their own successes.

- relate stories of other people's successes in overcoming obstacles.

- explain why resilience is essential for a fulfilling life.

- name the different components or four areas of personal resilience (body, mind, heart and soul).

- draw up an action plan for enhancing personal resilience.

Is it enough that the vulnerable patient survives the operation
and that the orphan survives the concentration camp,
or, in addition, should they not be able to run and laugh
and feel joy as well?

Dr George Vaillant (1993)

But is happiness a reasonable goal for us? Is it really possible
to be happy despite adversity? Is happiness a choice?

Yes, I believe that happiness can be achieved through the
training of the mind.

The Dalai Lama (2001)

Overview

What is resilience?

Resilience is sometimes simply defined as successful adaptation to risk and adversity. Some would define it as survival in the face of multiple challenges; others would describe it as coping with trauma.

We are born with an innate capacity for resilience, a so-called 'self-righting capability', which enables us to adapt to changing circumstances and develop:

- social skills
- problems-solving skills
- analytical-thinking skills
- autonomy
- a sense of purpose.

Jean Piaget, writing about the nature of intelligence, implicitly defines resilience when he says that it is 'knowing what to do when you don't know what to do'. And the great educator John Holt (1994) suggested to teachers that 'Since we cannot know what knowledge will be most needed in the future, it is senseless to try to teach it in advance. Instead we should try to turn out people who love learning so much and learn so well that they will be able to learn whatever needs to be learnt.'

It is also involves:

- having strategies for getting the best out of yourself – assuming that we live in a multiple intelligence world and that it is possible to develop the full range of your talents.
- loving learning.
- being able to keep going when things get tough.
- being resourceful (having a good, full 'toolkit' of techniques).
- adapting and responding to circumstances.
- having self-knowledge or knowing yourself.

For the purpose of this book, I have assumed that resilience is about:

- valuing yourself as a person.
- finding meaning and purpose in what you do.

- engaging in lifelong learning and developing a wide range of interests and skills.
- knowing how to deal with challenges and learning from them to become wise.
- persevering and adapting to circumstances to restore life balance.
- showing empathy and forgiveness.
- caring about others.
- maintaining a sense of humour, motivation and optimism.
- being happy.

Resilience is therefore much more than mere survival in the face of adversity, vulnerability and multiple risk factors. It should include healing, as well as growth and happiness. Overtly coping with circumstances is not good enough. Inner feelings of contentment are as important as the outward signs of functioning well. Hopefully, with experience, we grow stronger and wiser and develop a sense of gratitude and a deeper appreciation for the gift of what we call life. And, ultimately, we understand something about a collective purpose and the privilege of being able to make a difference.

If we could guide children in their growth process towards being resilient individuals, paradoxically we will co-create a much gentler, nurturing society. Highly resilient people are not invincible, tough and insensitive, but are committed and persevering, despite being vulnerable. Highly resilient individuals are also not self-centred, but show caring, deep concern for others, a need to contribute and to make a difference. Therefore, resiliency is not a programme, but rather a way of being engaged in this world. It is not only what we do that counts, but also how we do what we are doing.

Our ultimate need, according to Abraham Maslow is 'self-actualization'. In his theory about the hierarchy of human needs, self-actualization is our most advanced need, as shown in the diagram on page 11.

Self-actualization
- maximizing skills and ability
- realizing full potential

Esteem
- recognition
- esteem of others
- achievement

Belonging
- love
- affection
- companionship
- friendship
- family

Safety
- freedom from physical harm
- security from threatening events and surroundings

Physiological
- basic needs
- air
- water and food
- shelter
- warmth

Self-actualization means experiencing life fully, vividly, selflessly with full concentration and total absorption. At the moment of experiencing, the person is wholly and fully human.

Abraham Maslow (1954)

Self-actualization is a process, not a fixed state of being. It is a way of experiencing the world rather than a goal to be achieved – a way of staying centred in the present moment.

Abraham Maslow's hierarchy of needs addresses the needs of the individual – what do I need and what can I get. In one sense, it is self-centred in that it is focused on individual needs. Yet, by contrast, highly resilient individuals have a deep concern for others. In addition to Abraham Maslow's hierarchy of needs, Al Siebert (1996) suggests that highly resilient individuals have an additional need above the need for self-actualization, namely the need for synergy – the need that things should work out well for oneself as well as for others. This need requires a high level of emotional maturity – which means that our emotional needs go beyond our own needs, and extend to the needs of others. In Walter Anderson's words, 'The ability to look beyond ourselves' while respecting our own needs (1997).

Hardship and life's challenges can either be used to grow wiser and better, or cynical and bitter. Growth is a personal choice. People choose their reactions from moment to moment. Learned positive thinking can be promoted from an early age onwards, and if all of us develop the coping skills typical of highly resilient individuals when we are young, we create a healthier society.

Although individuals cannot always be completely balanced, they can restore life balance by being conscious of the different areas of their lives. This will enable people to understand where to invest more energy at a specific point in time. Like a tightrope walker balancing from side to side to eventually complete the challenging task, we could invest more energy and focus in some areas of our lives at the expense of others, while keeping in mind where we need to get to.

Resilience training for children aims to create that sensitivity or awareness regarding life balance.

Personal traits of resilient individuals

Based on extensive research findings, generic or general attributes typical of highly resilient individuals seem to be a combination of the following. They:

- have a strong sense of own identity.
- are able to manage themselves, handle stress and control impulses.
- can detach and distance themselves from dysfunction to be able to say: 'Bad things that happen to me, do not make me bad.'
- do not feel 'wounded' by attacks and can defer evaluation and judgement.
- are competent to perform a broad range of tasks (are multi-skilled) and use multiple intelligences.
- satisfy their curiosity over a broad spectrum of interests.
- assume internal locus of control to have an independent spirit and accept responsibility for their life and destiny.
- can function on their own and stay motivated.
- maintain a positive self-esteem belief in themselves and their abilities despite weaknesses or mistakes.
- accept and validate criticism when relevant and reject unwarranted criticism.
- feel comfortable with inner complexity and value their own paradoxical traits and use them to be flexible; for example, they can be critical and accepting, positive while anticipating what could go wrong, strong yet vulnerable, caring yet assertive and so on.
- see different perspectives and tolerate ambiguity and uncertainty.
- think flexibly.
- decide to play or relax when they need to.
- are durable and persistent – when the going gets tough the tough get going.
- remain hopeful and optimistic despite setbacks.
- feel difficulties are only temporary and rely on self-righting tendencies – the ability to recover from set-backs.

- have a positive attitude, a sense of purpose and a belief in a bright future.
- aspire to further lifelong learning and good results.
- establish and maintain spiritual connectedness.
- have faith that their life matters and show an active and meaningful engagement with the world.
- anticipate problems in order to avoid them, and expect the unexpected.
- trust intuition (gut feel) and accept it as a valid, useful source of information that they use in decision making.
- think reflectively to gain insight by learning from past experiences.
- experience inner peace and allow themselves to be transformed by experiences.
- establish and maintain secure, open, meaningful relationships with others.
- display responsiveness by eliciting positive responses from others and are resourceful in seeking help from others.
- show a perceptiveness by reading people well and adapt quickly to different personalities and situations.
- move comfortably between different cultures and are non-judgemental.
- show empathy.
- have a sense of humour, seeing the humour/fun in a situation, being able to laugh at themselves and share fun with others.
- can let go of anger and forgive others for mistakes.
- have problem-solving abilities and can think critically to find creative solutions to problems.
- think for themselves and question authority.
- show psychological plasticity by accepting inevitable situations or adapting to changing circumstances.
- adapt to changes in environment, self and others.
- decide to love unconditionally.
- can deal with difficult feelings.

Contrary to the general assumption that a Personality Type A person (a more driven, perfectionistic, task oriented and time conscious person) is more stress vulnerable than a Personality Type B person (a more people oriented, easy going, outgoing person), longevity studies have proven that each personality has its own shortcomings and is simply challenged by different things!

Perls and Silver (1999)

How learnable are resiliency traits?

This is possibly a question of whether personality traits are your genetic heritage or whether they are learnt – nature versus nurture.

From the author's perspective, personality is fixed – you are born with a tendency to be introverted or extroverted, to be more cognitive or to be more emotional in your approach to information, to be more comfortable with strong emotions, or to prefer dealing with tender or nurturing emotions.

Genetically you may be more prone to some ailments and illnesses. You can also be challenged by personal, family, economic, social, political, financial, educational and other difficulties. Some things are out of your control, such as war, natural disasters and other threats.

However, you can choose your reaction to life events. Life skills and emotional competencies can be learnt. The skills for expressing your own needs and opinions yet being willing to listen to others and understand their needs, the skills for making a presentation to a group, the skills for listening with empathy can all be acquired. It might take time and effort, but an extrovert can learn to keep quiet and listen with empathy and patience and an introvert can learn to actively take part in and manage group interaction. You can learn to think more flexibly and you can decide to adapt.

So, despite our natural tendencies, we can refine the skills that make us more effective in life. We can modify the hardware of our personalities with the software of emotional intelligence or personal and interpersonal skills. Therefore we may have our own first impulses or reactions to situations, but the wiser intelligence or inner wisdom of good judgement can override such impulses.

Emotional intelligence can be developed at any age, in any culture and in any stage of our lives. We can control our first impulses to act appropriately according to a wiser intelligence. Wisdom can be learnt!

Resilience is a book that offers the guidelines specifically for the development of a resilient mind.

Research into the inner nature of life's best survivors shows that a person can develop excellent mental health and emotional strength the same as physical health and physical strength.

Al Siebert (1996)

Guidelines
and
Activity Sheets

Guidelines: Activity Sheet 1

The talent game

Learning points

1 Resilient people develop multiple intelligences and are multi-skilled.
2 Resilient people have a sense of humour and maintain a healthy self-esteem even when they make mistakes.
3 Developing a range of interests and competencies allows us to live a fuller life.
4 Unique sets of talents make individuals different from each other and suitable for their specific purpose on earth.
5 Most of us can develop multiple intelligences to at least a certain level of competency.
6 Combinations of competencies are necessary for specific tasks. For example, whistling a tune requires a musical intelligence as well as small muscle movements; drawing a picture needs an artistic eye for colour, shape, texture and form, while the hands and fingers need to perform controlled movements, and the emotional expression through lines and colour gives the drawing character.
7 Resilient people are comfortable with the differences in people and are non-judgemental.

Comments

Both children need to complete each task before moving on to the next one. Ensure that learning partners support each other in task 3 when they stand on one foot with their eyes closed. You will need one or two soft balls, as children take turns at throwing a ball to partners in task 10. It may be a good idea to play lively music as the children work through all the tasks. When young ones stop having fun, they stop learning!

As a first activity, this is a distinct change from formal routine and is included to make the change in approach clear, right from the start.

Timing

3–5 minutes explaining the rules of the activity

10 minutes for both children to complete the activity

5–8 minutes concluding the activity with learning points and, as a group, reflecting on what the children have found out about themselves and others

1 *The talent game*

👥 Share in pairs

1 When you play this game, everybody has to do all the tasks.
2 Work with a partner. Make sure that you have both completed each task before moving on to the next one. Once you have completed a task, your partner has to make a tick (✔) in the box on the right.
3 You have 10 minutes to both complete the game.

Tasks   ✔

1 Sing a few notes from a well-known **song**...☐
2 Draw a picture of a **bicycle** in the space below. ....☐

3 **Stand on one foot** with closed eyes for 30 seconds without holding onto something..☐
4 Recite any **poem** to your learning partner. ....☐
5 Tell somebody about a **dream** you had during the past two weeks...............☐
6 What should the last **number** be: 33, 26, 19, 12, ?? ....☐
7 Describe another person's **personality**...☐
8 Say two things about **yourself** (your personality or how you behave) that everybody else will agree with. ....☐
9 Name your favourite **smell** or fragrance. ....☐
10 Hold your hands at your sides then **catch a ball** when it is thrown at you. ....☐

👥👥 Large group discussion

1 What did you find out about yourself?
2 What have you learnt about others?

Guidelines: Activity Sheet 2

Balancing my life

Learning points

A reflective activity that offers a further exploration of resiliency traits – if the essence of resilience is dynamic balance, we need to be conscious of all areas of our lives and think of ways to correct imbalances.

Comments

Children are welcome to discuss the outcomes of this activity with learning partners if they feel comfortable to do so.

It may be useful to discuss the individual items on the list as a large group discussion. Issues like right and wrong, what is healthy for me, asking for help and knowing where to go for assistance and so on may lead to interesting insights.

Timing

2 minutes explaining the principle of a balanced, full life

8 minutes self-evaluation

10 minutes discussing individual items, sharing ideas and feedback

2 Balancing my life

👤 Reflection

Read through the list below. Tick the boxes that you think suit you the best. Share with a learning partner what you have learnt from doing this activity.
You only need to talk about things you are comfortable to talk about.

	Do this already	Could do more
Mental		
1 Learning new things in school	☐	☐
2 Achieving success in school subjects	☐	☐
3 Spending time doing one or more hobbies	☐	☐
4 Finding out about things I am interested in	☐	☐
5 Being creative, like making something	☐	☐
6 Understanding the difference between right and wrong	☐	☐
7 Solving problems when they appear	☐	☐
Physical		
1 Breathing properly	☐	☐
2 Drinking healthy fluids, like water and fruit juice	☐	☐
3 Eating food that is good for me	☐	☐
4 Living in a safe and comfortable environment	☐	☐
5 Keeping my body fit	☐	☐
6 Working carefully with my money	☐	☐
7 Relaxing when I am tired	☐	☐
Emotional		
1 Having fun with friends and belonging to a group	☐	☐
2 Getting along with my teachers	☐	☐
3 Being safe with family	☐	☐
4 Feeling comfortable to do things on my own	☐	☐
5 Feeling part of our community	☐	☐
6 Talking to somebody I trust	☐	☐
7 Looking forward to learning new things	☐	☐
Spiritual		
1 Trusting my inner voice	☐	☐
2 Sitting quietly to think about my life	☐	☐
3 Knowing that I can make a difference	☐	☐
4 Practising a religion or meditating	☐	☐
5 Dreaming about my future	☐	☐
6 Feeling excited about next year	☐	☐
7 Believing that things will work out	☐	☐

👥 Questions for discussion in pairs

1 In which area of your life would you like to improve?
2 How many things can you change by yourself?
3 Are there some things you simply need to accept?
4 What do you need to ask help for?
5 Do you know who can help you when you need it? (Is there somebody that you can trust?)

The circle of life

Learning points

The Native American Indian metaphor is used as a short introduction to the different aspects of our lives that are to be balanced. It clarifies the different meanings. Ask the children what they think the metaphor means. Expand on the meanings.

Comments

1 The tree in the centre of the circle: the soul needs a variety of experiences to be fulfilled.
2 The East with light and peace: a sense of direction and guidance in life, right and wrong, possibly through religion or the teachings of caretakers or elders.
3 The South that brings warmth: relationships that make us feel protected, comfortable, safe and nurtured.
4 The West brings rain: uncomfortable but vital for growth – could mean challenges and learning, or new beginnings.
5 The North brings cold winds: hardship and adversity that make us strong and thankful for good times.

Read 'Self-reflection' from Activity Sheet 3 to the children, with pauses for reflection. Play soft music during this activity.

This activity is a preparation for Activity 4.

Timing

5 minutes overview

3 minutes reflection while reading the quote

5–8 minutes self-reflection

3 The circle of life

👤 On your own/ 👥 Share in pairs

The Native American Indians use a metaphor or short story to teach their children about resilience or balance in their lives. They believe that we need different experiences to make us happy, strong and fulfilled. When we have balance in our lives, we feel more comfortable with life and we are happier.

Study the picture below and read the quote by Joseph Brown. Then discuss with a learning partner how you understand the different parts of the picture.

The flowering tree was the centre of the hoop. From the east the tree received peace and light, the south gave warmth, the west gave rain, and the north with its cold and mighty wind gave strength and endurance.

Joseph Brown (1982)

👤 Self-reflection

Imagine you have to make a film or video about your life. Think of the different times in your life. Start with the time when you were a toddler; then the time before you went to school for the first time; your first year in school; and up to the present time. Think about your favourite games, the places you remember and the people you have met. Think about your parents, carers, family, best friends and teachers. How do you feel about it all? When you have finished the inner journey, make a drawing about your life using Activity Sheet 4.

Guidelines: Activity Sheet 4

My life

Learning points

This activity aims to create awareness of the different areas and needs in a person's life. If there is a high level of trust in the group, there will be spontaneous sharing. Otherwise, the activity offers the opportunity for self-reflection – a typical trait of a resilient person.

This is a sensitive activity and offers a good opportunity to engage the group in the task of setting ground rules for showing respect during such activities. List the ground rules on the board or a flipchart.

Comments

This is a private, reflective activity and the children are instructed not to make comments about their own or others' work. Only when they express a need to discuss their work should it be allowed. Ensure a respectful environment. Children need private space (enough space to work in, apart from each other, so that they sit on their own, without interference from others) and coloured pens or pencils to complete the spaces in the diagram. This is an opportunity to further connect to their personal experiences and how it affects them.

Timing

2 minutes explaining the activity

4 minutes laying ground rules

18 minutes completing the drawing or writing

2 minutes debriefing

4 *My life*

👤 On your own

Like the seasons in nature, we also experience seasons in our lives – good times, bad times, sad times, new beginnings. Think of your own life and draw pictures of your experiences in the spaces below.

1. What challenges me? When are things difficult for me? When am I unhappy or scared?
2. What makes me happy, calm or peaceful?
3. What makes me feel warm, safe and protected or part of a group? When do I feel that somebody is there for me?
4. What makes me feel uncomfortable and stretches me to have new experiences and learn new skills/things?

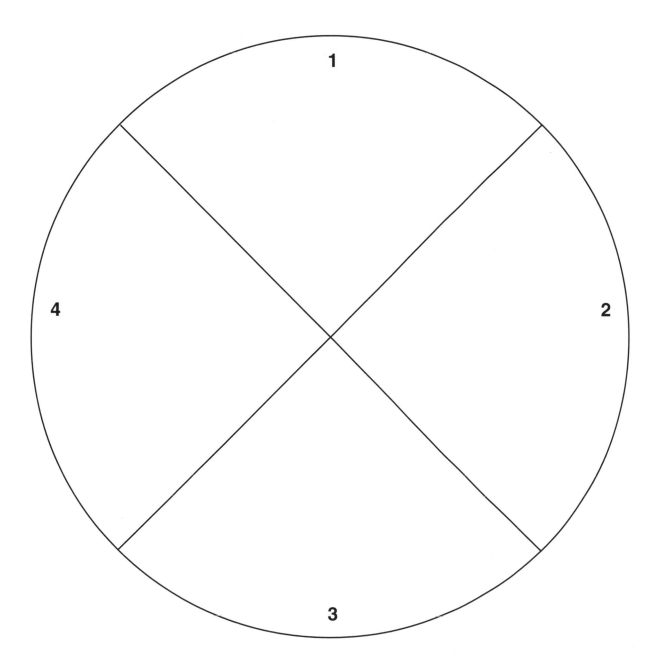

Guidelines: Activity Sheet 5

Mandla's story

Learning points

Ask a child to read Mandla's life story to the group. The story aims to point out how adversity can be overcome and how individuals can rise above their past.

Comments

1 Just as current successes cannot necessarily predict future successes, so past failures can be turned into future successes.
2 Each person has a choice in terms of how we react to life events and how we need to look out for each other.
3 Ask the children: 'When did you last go to a person sitting alone or looking miserable and comfort that person? It was because of other people's caring that Mandla received a scholarship to study. Sometimes we too need to help others.'
4 How do you feel when somebody else notices your discomfort and gives you support?
5 How does a lonely child who is not accepted in the 'in' group feel?
6 Why do peers hesitate to be associated with the outsider?
7 Who has guts? The person conforming to peer-group pressure, or the one that can act on their own?
8 What can you do when peer pressure becomes threatening?

Timing

10 minutes for reading the story and discussing the questions

5 Mandla's story

Mandla Khumalo was still very small when he and his parents had to flee from their country because of political unrest. When they arrived in South Africa his parents could not find work. They had no food and they could not afford a proper house.

Luckily somebody needed help on a cattle farm. During this time, the family lived with another family in a very small hut built out of mud. Mandla's mother cooked the little food they could find on an open fire outside the hut. After dinner they sat around the fire to keep themselves warm.

The hut was very cramped and everybody had to sleep where they could find some space to lie down in. There was no privacy and they seldom got a good night's rest, as there was always a lot of noise in the township.

Throughout Mandla's childhood, the family struggled to make a living. However, in high school he was one of the top students in his class, despite the fact that at home he had no space of his own in which to sit and do his homework.

Based on his good results and his excellent behaviour, he was granted a scholarship to go to university. He worked very hard and earned high marks. Eventually he graduated as a dentist.

Today Mandla Khumalo is a dental specialist with his own practice and works in his community as a highly respected professional. He inspires and advises many others in similar situations to overcome their limitations.

♟♟♟♟ Large group discussion

1 What do you do when things are really difficult?
2 What can you do when you experience problems?
3 What can you do when you notice that another person has problems?

Guidelines: Activity Sheet 6

The roles I play

Learning points

1 Interpersonal connection and cohesion (making contact with others and maintaining close, meaningful or trusting relationships) play an important role in being resilient.
2 Feeling a sense of belonging, experiencing support and being part of a group contribute to our happiness.
3 Understanding the role we play in other people's lives.
4 Having control over the quality and nature of a relationship.
5 Understanding how to contribute to others.

Comments

Read through the different sections in the table and explain to the group that this is about the way we see ourselves, and the expectations others have of us. However, we have a choice in terms of who and what we want to be. By thinking about their roles, children will realize that they have a role to play and it is up to them to shape that role. If they play additional roles, they may add these in too.

Timing

2 minutes introduction

10 minutes reflective self-assessment

5 minutes sharing in pairs or in small groups

2 minutes concluding

6 *The roles I play*

👤 On your own/ 👥👥 Share in pairs

Think of the different people in your life and how you form part of their lives. Write down a few words in each box. Then share your feelings about the role you play in each of the relationships with your partner.

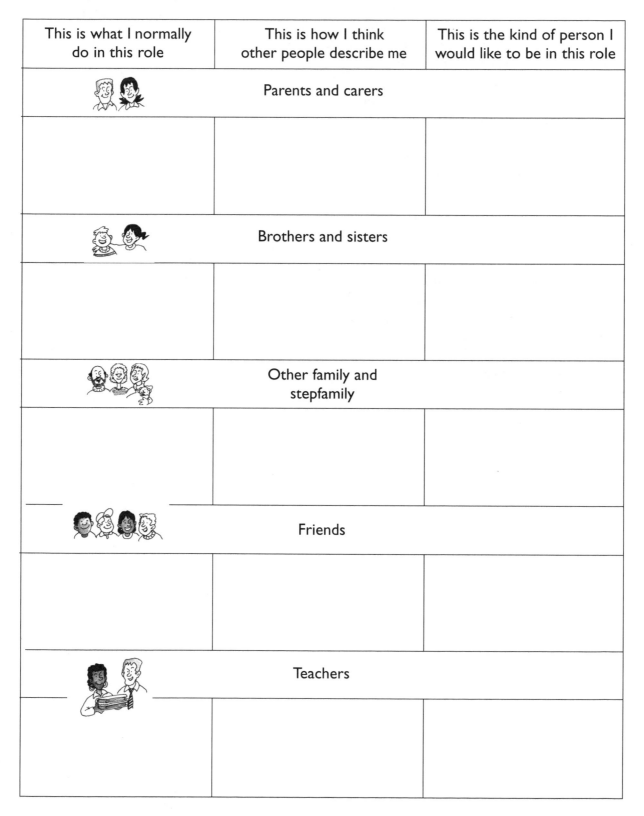

This is what I normally do in this role	This is how I think other people describe me	This is the kind of person I would like to be in this role
Parents and carers		
Brothers and sisters		
Other family and stepfamily		
Friends		
Teachers		

Guidelines: Activity Sheet 7

What makes me resilient?

Learning points

The concept of resilience is broad and difficult to define. Different researchers have different definitions. However, when we know what typical traits of highly resilient individuals are, we might understand the concept better and determine our own development needs. According to Dr George Vaillant (1993), 'We all know perfectly well what resilience is until we listen to someone else trying to define it.' To be able to list the attributes of highly resilient people is a good starting point.

Comments

For a greater understanding, compare this list of the typical traits of resilient individuals with the list in the overview on page 12 and give the children guidelines in terms of the meaning of the individual items. The children are encouraged to read through the list by themselves in order to understand the concept of being a resilient person. They use the list as a self-assessment and as a preparation for the next activity.

Timing

2 minutes explaining how to read through the list

8 minutes for silent self-assessment and clarification of items

7 What makes me resilient?

🧍 Reflection

This list is a summary of things resilient people are known for. Read through the list and ask yourself whether you could say these things about yourself. You do not need to discuss the list with others if it makes you feel uncomfortable. If you do not understand a sentence, ask the teacher to explain it to you.

Appreciating myself

1   I know myself well and can describe what type of person I am.
2   I can say 'no' to myself and to others.
3   I know that bad things happening to me do not make me bad.
4   I can do many things and I am interested in various things.
5   I know that I can make my life worthwhile.
6   I feel good about myself even though I might make mistakes.
7   I do not always feel exactly the same, and it is OK.
8   I can carry on even when some things change all the time.
9   I know when to play or to relax.
10 I keep on trying when things go wrong.
11 I feel good about the future.
12 I would like to keep on learning even after school.
13 I know that I am important and I can make a difference.
14 I know that there can be problems, so I plan to avoid them.
15 I listen to my inner voice – sometimes I just know what to do.
16 I learn from my mistakes.

Relating to other people

17 I have good friendships.
18 I ask for help when I need it.
19 I know what people want.
20 I am comfortable with people who are different from me.
21 I understand how other people feel and help where I can.
22 I can laugh at myself and have fun with others.
23 I forgive others for mistakes.

Relating to society

24 I find a way out and make plans when I have a problem.
25 I ask questions when I do not understand why I should do something.
26 I accept that some things cannot change and I have to make do.
27 I love people just as they are.

Guidelines: Activity Sheet 8

Defining resilience

Learning points

Based on the insights gained through all the worksheets completed so far, the children are encouraged by the activity sheet instructions to work in small groups to come up with a definition of their own.

Comments

Smaller groups finish their definitions and, at the end of the activity, each group gives feedback to the larger group.

Make notes on the board or flipchart, summarizing the ideas of the group as a whole.

Timing

6 minutes small group work to define resilience

9 minutes open discussion and listing of attributes

8 *Defining resilience*

👥👥👥 Small group discussion

Once you have read through the list of attributes of resilient people in Activity 7, you should have a good idea of what the word 'resilience' means. If you have to describe a resilient person to somebody else, how would you do it? In your small groups, work out your own definition of the word 'resilience' and write it on the 'notepad' below.

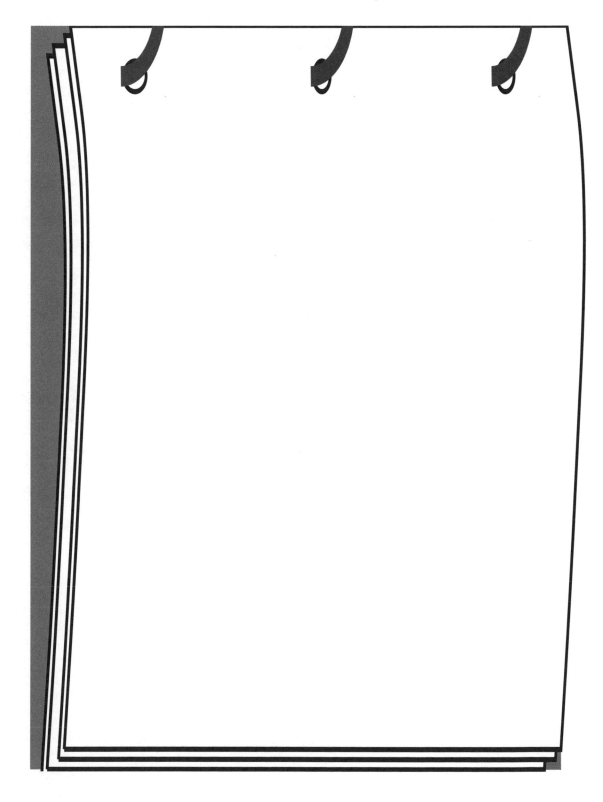

Guidelines: Activity Sheet 9

A letter to myself

Learning points

This activity promotes each child's self-reflection, self-appreciation and sense of responsibility for making the most of themselves and their abilities. It expands self-knowledge and builds self-esteem and self-appreciation.

Comments

This is a self-reflective activity that is explained beforehand. Hand out envelopes at the start of the activity and collect sealed, self-addressed envelopes at the end. Letters should be kept safe until they are handed out on completion of the resource book/syllabus. The idea is to notice progress, reinforce personal goals and make the activity personal and meaningful.

Timing

2 minutes explanation and handing out envelopes

12 minutes writing time

1 or 2 minutes for collecting envelopes

9 A letter to myself

♟ On your own

Write a letter to yourself about your good points, the kind of person you would like to be, the things that are important to you, your dreams and what you need to do more of to be even more resilient.

When you have completed this letter, put it in an envelope, write your name and address on the envelope and give it to the teacher.

You could write your letter like the one below .

Dear ....

(Write your own name here)

I am a person who is good at …

I would like to be …

Things that are important to me are …

My dreams are …

To be more resilient, I need to …

Yours truly,

....

(Write your own name here)

10 Action plan

The talents that I have are …	The talents that I need to develop are …
I should develop them further by …	What I need to accept is …
When I think of my life balance, I am happy with …	In order to be more balanced, I would like to do more …
Life experiences that I am thankful for are …	What I would like to change is …
What makes me resilient is …	I would like to be better at …
Roles that I enjoy are …	Roles that I would like to improve on are …
I will know that I am resilient when I …	I can help another person become more resilient by …

Marvellous me
I am unique

Outline

Outcomes

On completion of this unit, children should have the knowledge, skills and attitudes to:

- describe what is important to them.

- name their talents.

- say what they are good at.

- have a basic understanding of personality types.

- identify the characteristics of role models.

- explain why certain people are their role models.

- have insight into how they react to conflict situations.

- understand that different conflict situations require different approaches.

The turbulence of our times demands strong selves with a clear sense of identity, competence, and worth. With a breakdown of cultural consensus, an absence of worthy role models, little in the public arena to inspire our allegiance, and disorientingly rapid change a permanent feature of our lives, it is a dangerous moment in history not to know who we are or not to trust ourselves. The stability we cannot find in the world, we must create within our own persons.

Nathaniel Branden (1994)

Overview

In order to describe yourself as 'marvellous me', you should potentially know yourself, accept who you are, appreciate yourself, and rate yourself highly. All the above form part of what one could categorize as self-concept, self-knowledge, self-appreciation and self-esteem. It forms part of intrapersonal skills.

According to resilience theories, highly resilient individuals seem to have:

- a strong sense of own identity
- a positive self-image
- a healthy self-esteem.

Self-actualization

To become the best you can be takes more than talent and drive. You need to have opportunities – determined by others, or circumstances beyond your control.

Who you become is, therefore, a combination of many factors. Walter Anderson (1997) explains it as follows: 'If you were genetically capable of being the greatest long-distance swimmer who ever lived but unfortunately you were born two centuries ago to an Eskimo family in the northern reaches, it's a safe bet that you would never achieve your potential as a swimmer.'

Know yourself

How do you get to know yourself? You form your own perceptions of your personality, talents, capabilities and behaviours based on what you observe about yourself and what others tell you about yourself. Getting to know yourself is not an easy task. M. Scott Peck (1978) wrote: 'Greater awareness does not come in a single blinding flash of enlightenment. It comes slowly, piece by piece, and each piece must be worked for by the patient effort of study and observation of everything, including ourselves.'

The Johari window

The Johari Window is a well-known model created by Joseph Luft and Harry Ingham (Luft, 1963). It explains the role of interpersonal communication in the formation of your self-concept through self-disclosure, giving and receiving feedback, risk-taking, and consensual validation.

1 Transparent Area/Arena: Known to both self and others; for example, your name, age and physical appearance. The better your interpersonal relationships become, the bigger the transparent area becomes.
2 Blind Area: Things that others know about you, but you are unaware of; for example, mannerisms.
3 Hidden Area/Façade: Known to you but unknown to others; for example, private information, real feelings and so on.
4 Unknown Potential/Discovery Area: This is the area of potential discoveries about yourself. When taking on challenges you often discover and develop latent capabilities or characteristics within yourself.

Learning to grow

Group situations offer opportunities for self-assessment, self-disclosure, feedback, risk-taking and mutual agreement.

Self-assessment

Individual growth is encouraged through self-assessment and self-awareness. Group interaction provides opportunities for both.

Self-disclosure

Talking about yourself in a group setting is a form of disclosure, and sharing feelings with others can be healing. You choose what to reveal in accordance with your perceptions of what is appropriate in the situation and you are normally willing to share more in an atmosphere of trust.

Feedback

You will be more willing to listen to and act upon feedback from someone you know and trust. Because feedback can be constructive or destructive, it is important to follow the guidelines for giving and receiving feedback with care to ensure that it supports ongoing relationships.

Risk-taking

Taking on new challenges or sharing information about yourself are forms of risk-taking. When you experiment with new behaviour you may discover aspects of yourself that you may have been unaware of. The more comfortable you are with people, the more you are willing to risk sharing.

Mutual agreement

Feedback that supports/validates your observations is more powerful than individual feedback. You start to believe that you are intelligent (or stupid, or competent) when you hear that message from more than one person whom you trust. It can serve as a mechanism for 'correcting' your self-concept.

Self-concept and self-esteem

Self-concept refers to your view of yourself – it includes physical appearance, abilities, motives and social interaction with others.

You could be formed by:

- the environment – where you grew up.
- behaviour – how you act.
- ability – your talents and skills.
- beliefs – what you believe about yourself and lif in general.
- spirituality – how you think about your roles on earth, your purpose and life mission.
- your experiences of succeeding and failing.

Self-esteem refers to your rating of yourself. The following list may be helpful in clarifying aspects of self-esteem.

1 I find it easy to admit a mistake.
2 I find it easy to reach out to strangers.
3 I act according to my values, even if others don't approve.
4 I accept compliments comfortably.
5 I am myself around other people.
6 I accept myself, my faults and my weaknesses.
7 I know my strengths.
8 I can rejoice in someone else's achievements.
9 I don't compare myself to others.
10 I have peace of mind.
11 I believe I am unique and valuable.
12 I let my inner child play (I can be playful and innocent) without worrying about the reactions of other people.
13 I accept people who have different values.
14 I congratulate myself or others when any of us do well.
15 I can openly express my love for other people.
16 I love myself.
17 I accept all my feelings.
18 I am comfortable with myself when I am alone.

Self-esteem is not the same as being self-centred. In fact, Nathaniel Branden (1994) states that contrary to the belief that an individualistic orientation inclines you to antisocial behaviour, the opposite is true.

People with a highly developed sense of personal value and autonomy seem to display kindness, generosity, social co-operation and a spirit of mutual aid. In short, when I am OK, you are OK.

When you feel good about yourself, you tend to be more comfortable with others and are more likely to be sensitive to other people's needs and feelings and to acknowledge their strengths and talents. There is also the general assumption that when people feel good about themselves, they produce good results.

Self-esteem is enhanced when children:

- experience unconditional acceptance of their thoughts and emotions.
- feel valued as people.
- understand the boundaries they are allowed to function in.
- know that the boundaries are negotiable.
- are treated with respect and dignity.
- have parents with a high level of self-esteem.

Paradoxical traits

An important aspect in your appreciation of yourself is acceptance of your inner complexity – the fact that you may have opposing characteristics manifesting at different times and in different situations. Al Siebert (1996) pointed out how highly resilient people accept their inner complexity:

Self-actualized, highly resilient people achieve a paradoxical integration of many opposite traits, selfish unselfishness, flexible stability, pessimistic optimism, self-critical self-appreciation, loving anger, moral lust, cooperative non-conformity, responsible rebellion.

Seventeenth- and eighteenth-century philosophers Locke and Rousseau believed that babies came into the world as *tabula rasa* or 'blank slates', while society and the environment determined the basics of personality. And this view of personality has dominated educational systems leading us to assume that children are little vessels waiting to be filled up with facts.

We are more than the aggregate of our experiences. We are more than the quality of our nutrition. We are more than our genetic heritage. We are more than our biochemistry. And certainly, we are more than our parents' influence. We are created as unique individuals, capable of independent and rational thought that is not attributable to any source.

Dobson (1998)

The importance of taking responsibility for your own development and fulfilment is described by Walter Anderson (1997) as follows:

We define who we are every day, by the choices we make, and thus we choose who we want to be. We create ourselves. We invent ourselves. We are not what we eat – we are what we think.

Loving yourself

Loving yourself in this context means that you wholly accept yourself as you are. Facing everything about yourself and loving all of yourself – unconditional acceptance of who you are. It does not mean that you are self-righteous, or believe that you do not have needs in terms of personal growth or modification of your behaviour. It simply means that you are at peace with who you are.

Spiritual connectedness

One very prominent aspect of resilient individuals seems to be spiritual connectedness. It means that resilient people acknowledge different aspects of themselves. They accept that people are interdependent and that all living things are interconnected and form part of a bigger system and a collective spirit. One can also make the deduction that the spirit or soul is what we connect to when we feel centred and balanced. Thomas Moore describes

Odysseus	Demeter	Persephone
The father figure represents authority and wisdom and the power to direct his own life course. These strong leadership attributes are based on a natural inborn wisdom.	Like a typical mother, you can also demonstrate affection and empathy.	The inner child could be seen as vulnerable, ignorant and helpless. The child represents untapped potential.
Role functions		
mentor lead debate counsel make decisions	care love protect support negotiate on behalf of the child	be playful have innocence be creative be spontaneous
Experiences		
This part of the personality encourages the person to venture out, experience absence, longing, melancholy, separation, chaos and deep adventure.	This leads to experiences of deep emotional pain and sorrow	This creates the possibility of being abandoned, exposed to danger and fate.

the complexity of the soul by using three mythological characters to represent the three dimensions of soul.

> Modern psychology advocates that people need to be empowered to be healthy. But there are also times when we may need to be weak and powerless, vulnerable and open to experience. People need to be capable of intimacy – relationship is the ultimate goal. But soul also requires solitude and individuality.
>
> *Thomas Moore (1992)*

This means that to be fulfilled as a person, you need to be at peace with all of who you are and to be comfortable with being unique and even, at times, with being lonely.

Growing future employees

In the past, good children grew up to be desirable employees. They could be counted on to do what the boss told them and follow job descriptions until they retired.

Not anymore!

> What is needed today and demanded today, in the age of the knowledge worker, is not robotic obedience but persons who can think.
>
> *Nathaniel Branden (1994)*

The requirements for bringing up children have therefore changed. To prepare young people for the workplace, it makes sense to understand what will be required of them. Leadership theories have evolved over time, moving away from prescriptive authoritarian methods towards empowering styles and eventually to the modern servant-leadership theory. Respect is at the basis of this leadership style and, more than ever before, the leader is appreciated as a person and role model that needs to earn respect. Power is not situated in the position anymore, but rather in the person and the quality of the relationship.

This resource book offers opportunities to form that kind of relationship through structured interventions.

Guidelines
and
Activity Sheets

Guidelines: Activity Sheet 1

Pandora's box

Learning points

The objects we value or enjoy say a lot about us, our preferences and even our life stories.

Comments

The children are instructed to decorate a container and then take it home to collect objects of their choice. If they have valuable objects, they have to leave them at home and put a note in the container to represent the real object. The children should sit in circles in smaller groups or, if there is time, in a large group, and each one is given the opportunity to share the meaning or value of their objects with the group. This could be followed up by asking the group what they have learnt about each other.

Timing

2–3 minutes per child

5 minutes sharing what they have learnt about each other, themselves and the objects they value

1 Pandora's box

Individual activity for group work or home-play

Put your name on the lid of a cake/shoe box or brown paper bag and decorate it according to your taste. When you are at home, find six things that you really like and put them into the box. Bring the box with the items to the next workshop. You are going to explain to the group why you have chosen the specific objects and why they are special to you. If you don't feel like bringing valuable items with you, you can put a small piece of paper into the bag that describes the item you have at home. You may even collect objects like leaves, branches, pieces of bark and so on.

In the space below, make a few notes on what you appreciated about the other people in your group. What did they bring or say that you found inspiring or interesting? What have you learnt about yourself and the objects other people value?

Unit 2   Marvellous me

Guidelines: Activity Sheet 2

Who am I?

Learning points

What we think about ourselves is important, and other people's viewpoints sometimes help to provide a reality check.

Comments

The children sit in pairs and share the outcomes of their assessments. They give feedback to the larger group about the accuracy of their own assessments and how others sometimes appreciate qualities in us that we do not consider particularly special.

Close the session by explaining how important it is to think about our own development and to be tactful but honest when giving feedback to others. Also explain how we also form our perceptions about ourselves based on how others see us. Validation is important, especially if the feedback was less positive. Development is a lifelong venture.

Tip

It might be useful to make new pairings of children and to encourage friends to split up to allow more people to get to know each other and give honest feedback. Ensure that there is enough private space for each child to first complete their own assessment and then the learning partner's.

Timing

1 minute explanation

5 minutes rating themselves

5 minutes rating each other

5 minutes sharing ideas

2 Who am I?

👤 On your own/ 👥👥 Share in pairs

Read through the list below and decide how well you know yourself.
Tick either the 'yes' or the 'no' box.

		Yes	No
1	I know what I am good at..	☐	☐
2	I say what is important to me..	☐	☐
3	I say exactly what I feel..	☐	☐
4	I know what I want to achieve..	☐	☐
5	I am comfortable around people.......................................	☐	☐
6	I accept other people as they are	☐	☐
7	I feel good about myself, even if others criticize me...........	☐	☐
8	I can admit that I have made a mistake.............................	☐	☐
9	I can describe myself to others	☐	☐
10	I accept my body and the way I look................................	☐	☐

Ask a person that knows your fairly well and that you are comfortable with to complete the list below. They should do this according to how they experience you as a person. Fold over this top part of the activity sheet to allow the other person to answer their questions without any help. You may have a chat with the person afterwards to discuss the outcomes of the list and why the person has this opinion about you.

Your name _____

1	Knows what he/she is good at..............................	☐	☐
2	Says what is important to him/her........................	☐	☐
3	Says exactly what he/she feels	☐	☐
4	Knows what he/she wants to achieve...................	☐	☐
5	Appears to be comfortable around people............	☐	☐
6	Accepts other people as they are.......................	☐	☐
7	Feels good about him/herself even if others criticize him/her...	☐	☐
8	Admits mistakes..	☐	☐
9	Can describe him/herself	☐	☐
10	Seems to be comfortable with his/her body and the way he/she looks...................................	☐	☐

Guidelines: Activity Sheet 3

Talents, skills and interests

Learning points

Our skills and combination of skills enable us to function in certain jobs more successfully and happily than in others. A career choice is not easy to make and the more we are aware of what we like and what we are capable of, the better we can decide.

Comments

The children are instructed to read through the table and mark the blocks they feel represent their current skills and interests. They then circle potential areas for development. At the end of the activity, a general discussion is held to share insights. You could also add up the total number of children having a particular skill and compile a talent bank simply for interest's sake.

Tip

This is not a test, but rather a thought-provoker.

Timing

1 minute briefing

5–10 minutes self-study

5 minutes general discussion

5 minutes compiling talent bank

2 minutes wrapping up

3 Talents, skills and interests

👤 On your own

Tick any of the items below that are true for you. Circle any skills you would like to learn.
There are some empty boxes so that you can add to the list if you wish.

Play a musical instrument	☐	Make things with my hands	☐	Combine tastes to make food	☐	Decorate a room	☐
Sing	☐	Play sports	☐	Decorate a cake	☐	Use colours well	☐
Write music or songs	☐	Dance	☐	Smell things well	☐	Know how to dress well	☐
Hear sounds and faint noises	☐	Balance my body, as in gymnastics	☐	Cook food	☐	Arrange flowers	☐
Draw pictures	☐	Console or calm people down	☐	Think differently about things	☐	Mend things with my hands	☐
Do fine work with my fingers	☐	Encourage people	☐	Understand maths	☐	Fix things or put things together	☐
Write beautifully	☐	Listen to people's problems	☐	Solve problems quickly	☐	Grow plants	☐
Make sculptures	☐	Bring people together	☐	Come up with interesting ideas	☐	Do woodwork or assemble models	☐
Make speeches	☐	Give people advice	☐	Act	☐	Do business or sell things	☐
Negotiate or argue a point	☐	Help people with problems	☐	Amuse people by being funny	☐	Calculate numbers	☐
Convince others of my idea	☐	Explain things to people	☐	Play tricks or do magic	☐	Understand how computers work	☐
Organize people	☐	Help others to make peace	☐	Make funny drawings	☐	See fine detail	☐
Know and care about animals	☐	Estimate distance between places	☐	Know what is going to happen	☐	Run fast or react very fast	☐
Study sea life	☐	Find my direction when travelling	☐	Plan ahead	☐	Jump high	☐
Work with nature	☐	Compare sizes accurately	☐	Have a gut feel for the right decision	☐	Swim well	☐
Be interested in the weather (storms)	☐	Know what will fit into a space	☐	Take chances that work out fine	☐	Throw things accurately	☐
Have a strong body	☐		☐		☐		☐
Use my muscles for a long time	☐		☐		☐		☐
Run long distances	☐		☐		☐		☐
Use my arms to throw things	☐		☐		☐		☐

Guidelines: Activity Sheet 4

Role models

Learning points

We can learn from others.

Comments

Instruct the children to write down their words representing the qualities of their role models. List the qualities on the board. Discuss the relevance of having a role model. Discuss the responsibility of being a good role model and ask the group to consider the impact of a negative role model on young people and society as a whole.

Timing

5 minutes self-reflection and listing words on activity sheet

5 minutes general discussion

4 Role models

♟♟♟♟ Large group activity

Think of a well-known person you admire. What makes the person so special? Write down all the things you would like to be true for you too, such as *forgiving*, *beautiful*, *kind*, *strong* or *friendly*. You will never be exactly like the person you admire, because every person is unique, but you can learn from others and other people can inspire you.

My role model is _____

I would like to be like him/her because he/she is:

Guidelines: Activity Sheet 5

Personality

Learning points

If we understand different personalities, we can treat people according to their personal needs.

Comments

The children assess themselves and colour blocks that feel like them. If they colour most of the blocks, it is OK because we are supposed to be flexible and adaptable in our approach. While the children rate themselves, draw four squares on the board with Facts, Methods, Ideas and Relationships written on top. When they are finished with their self-assessments, the children write their names in the block representing their highest rating in red and the second highest rating in blue. Talk about the number of names per category and how we need to be tolerant of people who are different from us, although we naturally like people who are like us.

Tip

This is not a test, merely a structured tool to guide thoughts and further discussions.

Timing

5 minutes self-rating

10 minutes summarizing, categorizing and discussing

1 minute concluding

5 Personality

🖕 On your own

Read through the table below. What feels like you?

Colour each block that feels like you. When you have done that, count the number of blocks you have coloured in each column.

Now rate the columns by writing down 1, 2, 3 and 4 in the space at the bottom of the list, with 1 being the column that feels most like you and 4 being the column that feels least like you.

Ideally, we should be able to do all of what is in the table, but we naturally tend to like some things more or find some things easier to do. Write your first and second choice in the appropriate space on the board.

Using the same table, ask your family members how they see themselves, and then discuss with them what you appreciate about each other.

Facts	Methods	Ideas	Relationships
1 Enjoy working with facts	1 Do things step by step	1 Enjoy dreaming	1 Love to make peace
2 See the small parts	2 Follow rules	2 Find the things that are similar in situations and in people	2 Enjoy talking to others
3 Notice the things that do not fit in	3 Use a specific methods to do things	3 Enjoy change and new challenges	3 Like to work with people and be part of a group
4 Like things to be precise	4 Like to plan things ahead	4 Like to try new things	4 Care about other people
5 Am more comfortable with thinking than with dreaming or feeling	5 Want to know if something can really work	5 Do things in a way that is different from most other people's methods	5 Can listen to other people's problems
Total	Total	Total	Total

Guidelines: Activity Sheet 6

What kind of animal are you?

Learning points

People have preferred conflict styles based on their experience and personalities. However, different conflicts need different approaches and one can learn how to handle conflict more productively.

Comments

Begin by asking the children: 'If you were an animal, which animal would you like to be?' Then ask: 'Why did you choose that animal? What do you like about the animal of your choice?' The children share this within the larger group.

For the second part of this activity, ask the children to select one of the five animals depicting conflict styles, choosing the one that represents themselves best. They share their choices and reasons for their choices within the small groups. Finish the activity by asking the children what they have learnt about each other and how it is going to help them.

Timing

30 seconds –1 minute per child during the first part of activity

3 minutes selecting conflict style

5 minutes small group activity

2 minutes wrapping up

6 *What kind of animal are you?*

⁙ Large group activity

Think of yourself when you have a problem with another person. If you were an animal, what animal would you like to be when you are in conflict? Why?

⁙ Small group activity

Select one of the following animals that you feel best represents you when dealing with conflict. Discuss your choice, and reasons for your choice, with your group.

The Turtle

Turtles do not like conflict – it makes them feel helpless. They would rather give up something than fight for it.

The Shark

Sharks feel proud of themselves when they win. Winning is so important to them that they will give up friendships to get what they want.

The Teddy Bear

Teddy Bears try to avoid conflict in case someone gets hurt. Friendship is very important to them.

The Fox

Foxes prefer to compromise (meet the other person halfway). They are willing to give up something and they expect the other person to also give up something in order to make peace.

The Owl

Owls want to solve problems in such a way that everybody is satisfied. Although they will not rest until the problem is solved, friendship is important to them and they will therefore be careful with their words.

Based on Geri McArdle (1995)

Guidelines: Activity Sheet 7

I am ...

Learning points

It is not easy to describe ourselves, and by doing this activity young people become aware of themselves and their unique set of qualities. This activity is important for forming a realistic self-concept and self-appreciation.

Comments

Using coloured pens and pencils, water colours, clippings from magazines and so on, the children design their own emblems or logos. The sharing of something that not a lot of people know about is based on the Johari window concept of self-disclosure and risk-taking, which requires people to respect each other and to treat the information shared with respect.

Timing

20 minutes designing emblem

1–2 minutes per child sharing with group

2 minutes closure

7 I am ...

👤 On your own

Use the emblem below, or draw your own emblem of yourself. It is similar to the logo of a company, or a family emblem. It represents you and says something about yourself.

- Write your name in the space on the ribbon. If your name has a special meaning, write that down as well. Was there a reason why you were given a specific name?

- In the space on the left of the emblem, list or illustrate a few things you are good at.

- In the space on the right of the emblem, list or illustrate something about yourself that not many people know and that might come as a surprise to them.

- Explain to the larger group what your emblem means.

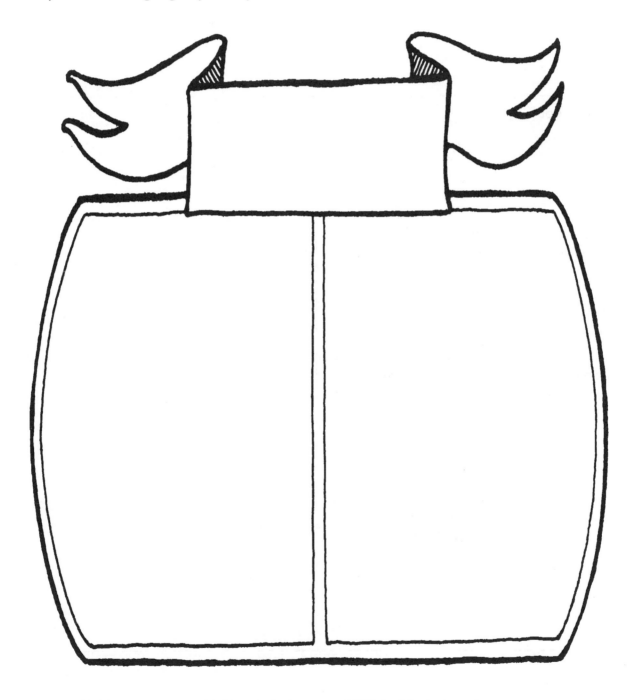

8 Action plan

Challenges	How, Where and When
Learn more about myself	
Master more skills	
Have a hobby	
Understand more about other people's personalities	
Grow my own self-esteem by taking on new challenges	
Build another person's self-esteem by acknowledging the person's good points	

Emotions

I say what I feel

Outline

Outcomes

On completion of this unit, children should have a better understanding of their emotions and notice how their emotions make them behave. To be able to handle their emotions better children should be able to:

- notice different emotions.

- give their emotions names.

- understand why they feel like they do.

- say how they feel in a proper way.

- allow themselves to feel emotions instead of pretending they do not exist.

- use the pause button when they experience strong emotions.

- care about other people's emotions.

- learn how to say they are sorry when they hurt someone else.

Being emotionally intelligent means that you know what emotions you and others have, how strong they are, and what causes them. Being emotionally literate means that you know how to manage your emotions because you understand them.

Claude Steiner with Paul Perry (1997)

Overview

As children grow ever smarter in IQ, their emotional intelligence is on the decline. Perhaps the most disturbing single piece of data comes from a massive survey of parents and teachers that shows the present generation of children to be more emotionally troubled than the last. On average, children are growing more lonely and depressed, more angry and unruly, more nervous and prone to worry, more impulsive and aggressive.

Robert Cooper and Ayman Sawaf (1998)

Stephen Covey (1997) summarized problems in schools as follows:

Top disciplinary problems according to public school teachers

1940	1990
Talking out of turn	Drug abuse
Chewing gum	Alcohol abuse
Making noise	Pregnancy
Running in the halls	Suicide
Cutting in line	Rape
Dress-code infractions	Robbery
Littering	Assault

Many of the behaviours described above could be translated into actions resulting from insensitivity towards others, or as alexthymia (emotional numbness – not feeling at all). Maybe it is the result of uncontrolled anger and resentment. Or it could be a misguided outcry to fight feelings of loneliness and despair. Or…? Who knows exactly why children are acting in the way they do? Where does it leave children and their teachers?

Maybe the biggest challenge for teachers and education today is not to teach, but to develop young people, because knowledge alone is not enough to make you successful, well-adjusted or happy in life.

Defining emotional intelligence

Emotional intelligence is a term often heard in the field of human development. Each author on the subject probably has a unique frame of reference from which they are able to address or clarify the issue. It may be useful to consider a few definitions, each offering a different approach to the subject.

Claude Steiner (1997) places strong emphasis on the identification and description of emotions, understanding what causes them and knowing how to handle them. He defines it as:

Being emotionally intelligent means that you know what emotions you and others have, how strong they are, and what causes them. Being emotionally literate means that you know how to manage your emotions because you understand them.

Because people often interpret the same words differently, we could be talking to each other in the same language and still have misunderstandings. Confucius said that words are such poor conveyers of meaning that it is a wonder if two people ever understand each other. So David Ryback's (1996) definition highlights the importance of catching the emotional meaning of a message:

Emotional Intelligence is best defined as the ability to use your awareness and sensitivity to discern the feelings underlying interpersonal communication, and to resist the temptation to respond impulsively and thoughtlessly, but instead to act from receptivity, authenticity and candour.

His definition also emphasizes:

- the concept of impulse control – thinking before we act.

- being open and sensitive to other people's realities.

- being true to ourselves.

- being honest – saying what we mean and meaning what we say.

Robert Cooper and Ayman Sawaf (1998) define emotional intelligence as:

> The ability to sense, understand, and effectively apply the power and acumen of emotions as a source of human energy, information, connection and influence.

In this definition emotions are described as a useful source of information that add additional insights to pure facts, enhance or strengthen our relationships with others, and give us the power to make a difference. Emotions are sometimes described as movement through energy. When we connect with people on an emotional level, we are more likely to engage their interest and convince them of our standpoint and so influence their actions or behaviour.

Although the study of emotions or feelings is often called emotional intelligence, it can also be referred to as emotional literacy. Frances Wilks (1998) wrote:

> Emotional Intelligence is applied Emotional Literacy, and these terms, although not synonymous, amount to much the same thing in practice.

Whatever the formal definition may be, most authors agree that being able to manage your emotions in a productive way and understanding other people's emotions leads to improved self-esteem and better relationships.

Workplace competencies

Today's employers have sophisticated requirements. Emotional competencies are being measured as part of performance management in many companies.

The reason for this is that self-management and teamwork are essential for getting work done. The diagram below explains the difference between the various skills needed to perform well at work.

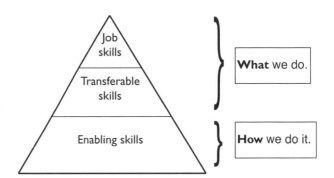

Job-specific skills are about work content, and equip a person to do a specific job. For example, a dentist has to be able to fix a broken tooth. This specialized ability may not be necessary for other jobs. Most of our training after school is about job-specific skills.

Transferable or *functional skills* are applicable to a variety of work situations and are based on reading, writing and arithmetic. Many of these skills are taught at school.

Enabling skills or life skills are necessary to cope with life in general. These skills are selectively included in our formal education, yet they are critical in most spheres of life and include a variety of emotional competencies.

According to J. A. Rosenkranz (quoted in Crane, 2000):

> Your education has been a failure no matter how much it has done for your mind, if it has failed to open your heart.

Therefore, successful learning is about being comfortable with yourself and managing yourself as well as about caring and getting along with others. When we strive to develop resilient learners, it would be unrealistic not to develop emotional intelligence as part of the enabling skills. As Daniel Goleman (1998) states:

IQ alone at best leaves 75 percent of job success unexplained, and at worst 96 percent – in other words, it does not determine who succeeds and who fails.

Emotional competencies (personal and interpersonal competencies) are important for career advancement and form the underlying skills of leadership development programmes in corporate companies. Today these competencies are crucial, because of the shift in requirements for being a good leader. Robert Hawley (quoted in Ryback, 1998) sums it up as follows:

The twentieth century leader is somebody who tends to have strong but hard personal qualities, somebody who is arrogant but inspiring. However, twenty-first century leaders will be those who can demonstrate a greater empathy and concern for people issues and those who do not rely on position or rank for their status.

Emotional competencies form groups or clusters and can include the following:

- Personal skills
  - › self-knowledge, (knowing and understanding ourselves)
  - › self-appreciation (valuing and accepting ourselves and having good self-esteem)
  - › self-management (controlling our actions, time and stress)
  - › self-motivation (applying internal locus of control and taking initiative).
- Interpersonal skills
  - › empathy (understanding and caring about others)
  - › group skills (understanding how to be part of a team, manage conflict and so on).
- Organisational skills
  - › leadership (leading, mentoring, coaching, mediating, counselling, negotiating and so on that are advanced applications of personal and interpersonal skills and political savvy).

These skills were previously described as so-called 'soft skills' and were viewed as the 'nice to haves' but 'not essential' for job competence. However, modern leaders have discovered that knowledge can become obsolete, and that lifelong learning is part of being effective in your job. What is crucial for career success is to be able to manage and motivate yourself while being sensitive and inspirational to others. Emotional competencies give people personal power, which goes way beyond formal job descriptions. In fact, it is when things go wrong or when there are changes in the work set-up that emotional competencies distinguish the winners from the average. Emotional competencies help people to persevere and demonstrate staying power.

Emotions and health

The relationship between emotions and health has long been a point of discussion. This relationship is clearly explained in many books, some written by medical doctors. Candace Pert (1997) wrote:

We must take responsibility for the way we feel. The notion that others or circumstances can make us feel good or bad is untrue. Consciously or – more frequently – unconsciously, we are choosing how we feel at every single moment. The external world is in so many ways a mirror of our beliefs and expectations. Why we feel like we feel is the result of the symphony and harmony of our own molecules of emotion that affect every aspect of our physiology, producing blissful good health or miserable disease.

If it is true that emotions play such an important part in our well-being, the question would be whether we could learn to understand and manage emotions and at what age we should attempt to master emotional skills. The following viewpoints clarify the issue:

Fortunately, scientists now consider EQ a learnable intelligence, one that can be developed and improved at any time and any age.

Daniel Goleman (1998)

Research into the inner nature of life's best survivors shows that a person can develop excellent mental health and emotional strength the same as physical health and physical strength.

Al Siebert (1996)

Reflex: primitive reactions to threat

When we feel threatened (or are actually threatened), we are more likely to revert to 'survival mode' for which fight, flight, freeze or flock are typical outcomes. Reflexes during stress include the following:

Fight
- Attacking
- Being jealous
- Being hostile
- Blaming
- Complaining
- Throwing 'Hissy-fits'.

Flight
- Running away physically
- Hiding behind closed doors
- Being late, absent or on sick leave
- Clinging to old dreams and rules
- Longing for the good old days
- Taking part in gripe sessions
- Becoming too self-absorbed to notice other people's problems
- Experiencing pain or problems feel overwhelming
- Feeling life is unfair since you deserve better treatment and immediate relief.

Freeze
- Being stunned, cannot think clearly
- Forgetting deadlines
- Having accidents
- Feeling miserable
- Considering no support as enough
- Viewing the future as bleak or blank
- Blaming and acting like a passive victim
- Hoping someone else will 'fix it'
- Alternating panic with apathy, lethargy and depression.

Flock
- Spending excessive time with friends
- Being co-dependent – when people are being overly reliant on each other for emotional support
- Joining the dominant group
- Disregarding a personal value system to fit in with a group
- Submitting to group pressure
- Avoiding being alone.

Stress reflexes therefore lead to actions that could be described as aggressive, submissive or passive instead of assertive. If our emotional reactions get out of hand, we normally regret our words and actions afterwards, or resent our lack of response, which in turn leads to the development of poor self-esteem.

Modifying reflex with emotional intelligence

If we are emotionally intelligent, we can change reflex or pure uninhibited reactions into a response. Response is the result of a conscious decision based on our judgement of a situation. In a way, you could describe 'response' as using head and heart – integrating thinking and feeling.

While reflex may be an over-emotional reaction, response is a modified, toned-down reaction that is more compatible with who we are and our beliefs and values as well as the requirements of the situation. It means that during high stress we put our impulsive reaction on hold until we have processed the emotion to such a level that our responses contribute to the outcome we want to achieve. This delay in reaction is what Stephen Covey (1994) describes as the 'pause button'. In resilience theory, related terminology is 'impulse control' and 'delay of gratification'.

> Fear and pain should be treated as signals not to close our eyes, but to open them wider.
>
> *Nathaniel Branden (1994)*

Six steps in processing emotions

> When we fight a block, it grows stronger. When we acknowledge, experience, and accept it, it begins to melt.
>
> *Nathaniel Branden (1994)*

Apart from understanding our emotions and what caused them, we need to 'work on them' in order to move on. Emotions do not just go away when we ignore or suppress them. Over time, accumulated negative emotions cause harmful effects.

The ideal is to learn useful lessons from experiences and make them part of our frame of reference. When we use our experiences to become wiser, more tolerant, tactful and happy they have served a good purpose.

Dealing successfully with our emotions implies several steps.

1 Become aware of the emotions and acknowledge them.
2 Express the emotions and determine what caused them.
3 Allow yourself to fully experience the emotion, even physically.
4 Let go of the emotions to make them part of your history.
5 Learn something from the experience.
6 Move on, wiser.

If we do not allow ourselves to experience emotions but ignore, suppress or postpone them, they do not go away. We merely accumulate and store emotions to form a block that, unfortunately, not only makes one ill or stressed, but also blocks out joy and happiness.

Using emotions productively

One night a young man's mother asked him to make a phone call from the telephone booth across the street from their flat. They had no telephone in their house at the time.

When the young man finished his call, he replaced the receiver. Suddenly he noticed that his hand felt damp. He inspected his hand under the street lamp – it was covered in blood. He touched his face with the other hand and found more blood.

He was not bleeding, but whoever had used the phone before him had been hurt or wounded. This was not unusual in the neighbourhood this young man grew up in.

The young man stepped into the street looking up and down for the wounded person, but there was nobody in sight. Then he ran across the street and up the stairs until he reached the door of their small flat. He nervously opened it, stepped inside and ran to the kitchen sink. He quickly washed the blood from his face before his mother could see it because he did not want to upset her.

Later on, as he sat alone on the balcony, he wondered about the unknown person whose blood had covered his face.

Then he became angry!

'I'm getting out of here!' he promised himself. And, for the first time in his life, he really meant it. This man was Walter Anderson, who became a successful businessman and motivational speaker.

> *Inspired by Walter Anderson (1997)*

This man used emotions productively! Anger, like other so-called negative emotions, can be a source of positive energy if we use it to change circumstances for the better instead of acting like a victim while criticizing or blaming others.

Bullies are actually big babies

Although bullies use fear, power, cruelty and threats to control others, they are actually people of low self-esteem. They victimize people who appear weak and passive, and ensure that they have enough supporters of their own.

One strategy to deal with them is to let them vent their anger, while you refrain from retaliating or reacting. If you could absorb their anger and appear to be unaffected by it, you are in a better position to confirm that you understand their viewpoint. It is best to deal with them in public, as opposed to the normal strategy of dealing with emotional issues in private. Deal with them immediately and in public.

When children display unacceptable social behaviour, such as violence, bullying, robbery, physical or sexual abuse of others, they are in effect communicating to their parents a need for recognition and unconditional acceptance. Very often children from dysfunctional homes hide their deep hurt by using aggressive behaviour. Adverse circumstances at home alienate children from others, and even a reprimand is better than no attention at all. By bullying others, they release their resentment, anger and hurt, and confuse the fear of others with respect and admiration – which they wrongfully attempt to earn.

How does a school manage bullies?

Do bullies get the kind of recognition they crave, or are they handled in a way that makes them even more desperate for attention? By punishing or ignoring bullies, they are not given the kindness, acceptance and attention they desperately seek. In essence they feel that they are not good enough, and the strategy

the school applies should not reinforce that feeling of unworthiness.

Are those who display sensitivity and kindness towards others acknowledged and rewarded?

Are those who stand up for others encouraged and supported?

John Barnes, general manager of SASOL Polymers South Africa, once made the following comment: 'Almost every problem with a child could be solved with loving attention.'

Those who make it very difficult for us to love and accept them are those who need our love and acceptance most desperately. How willing are we to listen with the intention of understanding, accepting, guiding and kindness?

Guidelines
and
Activity Sheets

Guidelines: Activity Sheet 1

Body language

Learning points

When you start to notice your own body language and other physical movements or reactions when experiencing certain emotions, you can progress to handling the emotion itself and acting appropriately. Body movement can act as an 'early warning system' because, before you consciously realize you are experiencing the emotion, it could manifest itself in your physical body. It also helps to notice or read other people's emotions – without them saying anything – thus allowing you to approach other people in accordance with their emotional state.

Comments

Explain to everyone that the activity is about each of us being aware of ourself, how we feel and what we do. Name examples of how people could act differently even though they experience the same emotions. Sometimes our emotions and actions are not congruent (do not match). For example, you could be happy yet tears could be streaming down your face.

Arrange the children in smaller groups of three or four sitting in different areas of the room, with adequate space between each group. The children take turns to role play experiencing certain emotions. At the end of the activity, point out the similarities and differences between people and the way they handle emotions.

Tip

Use background music if possible. This is supposed to be a light-hearted activity.

Timing

2 minutes explanation

15 minutes role play

5 minutes coming out of role play, and general discussion

1 Body language

👥👥👥 Small group role play

To perform this activity, each person in the group acts like they usually do when they are:

- **Angry**
- **Sad**
- **Scared**
- **Happy**
- **Disappointed**

During the role play, take note of other group members' eyes, mouth, hands, feet, voice and body movements. At the end of the activity, explain to the group what you have noticed about each other.

Guidelines: Activity Sheet 2

House of emotions

Learning points

Emotions vary in intensity as well as their influence on ourselves and others. Some emotions are very mild and barely noticeable. Other emotions are strong and easy to recognize. Just as emotions vary in intensity, they could have their own 'colour'. You could therefore pretend that emotions are like a colour chart consisting of different colours and shades. Some emotions are associated with specific colours, but cultural differences can influence such associations. For the purpose of this activity, the children are encouraged to give their own interpretation of emotions, with the purpose of enhancing their awareness. Emotions can:

- attract people; for example, when we are happy.
- drain people of energy; for example, when we are depressed.
- push people away; for example, when we are angry or frustrated.

When we can name our emotions, we are in a better position to process them and to understand the reactions of other people.

Comments

Use the diagram (House of emotions) and 'talk through' the different 'rooms' by reading the list of emotions in each room and asking which word represents the strongest emotion in the list and which one the most subtle. In a large group discussion, explore the different emotions and how they make us feel. Then instruct the children to draw faces that match the emotions in the respective rooms, and shade or colour the rooms in the colour that they associate with the emotion in each room. Lastly, they have to draw a face that represents their favourite emotion in the roof part of the house. Make it clear that this is an activity of personal expression and that no two people experience it in exactly the same way. There are no right or wrong faces and colours, and instead of being critical, they may prefer to share within small groups what their reasoning was in making their choices for faces and colours.

Tip

As an ice-breaker, you could hold up different coloured scarves or material samples and ask the children to share their interpretation of the colour; for example, why do matadors carry red or bright pink capes?

Timing

3 minutes introduction

2 minutes general discussion

5 minutes for the children's activity

5 minutes larger group discussion and conclusion

2 House of emotions

👤 On your own

1 For each room in your house of emotions, draw a little face that expresses the emotion described in that particular room. Then colour the rest of the room in a colour that you think suits the emotion. (There is no right or wrong colour or face – this is the way you experience it.)

2 Draw a face that expresses your favourite emotion in the roof part of the house.

Happy	Caring	Depressed
Thrilled	Like	Bad
Excited	Cherish	Sad
Great	Idolize	Awful
Good	Respect	Horrible
Fine	Worship	Despair
Cheerful	Friendly	Gloomy
Fantastic	Devoted to	Miserable
Marvellous	Adoration	Unhappy
Wonderful	Attached to	Disappointed

Guilty	Fearful	Confused
Exposed	Terrified	Puzzled
Ashamed	Panicky	Troubled
Guilty	Afraid	Unsure
Regretful	Scared	Bothered
Wrong	Anxious	Foggy
Crummy	Jumpy	Mixed up
Sick at heart	Shy	Uncomfortable
Embarrassed	Frightened	Going around in circles
Responsible for	Paralyzed	Uncertain

Hurt	Angry	Lonely
Used	Furious	Isolated
Crushed	Infuriated	All alone
Wounded	Violent	Forsaken
Devastated	Bitter	Remote
Humiliated	Hateful	Cut off
Rejected	Irritated	Let out
Laughed at	Mad	Excluded
Unappreciated	Spiteful	Lonesome
Taken for granted	Cross	Abandoned

Guidelines: Activity Sheet 3

Where in my body do I feel emotions?

Learning points

Emotions manifest themselves in the body. Different emotions affect different parts of the body. By being aware of the bodily sensation, the emotion can be accessed. Think of some well-known idioms describing emotions/feelings. Some examples are:

- butterflies in the stomach
- lead in my feet
- heart torn in two
- being breathless
- pain in the neck
- feel it in my bones
- blood rushing to my head.

Each of the expressions are linked to a specific emotion or combination of emotions. For instance, 'Lead in my feet' would be an indication of a feeling of uncertainty or a lack of motivation.

Comments

Explain to the group how our emotions influence the way we feel in our bodies and affect our **energy levels**. For example, if you **dread** an event, you will feel **tired**, but if you think of something that really **excites** you, you would be **energized**. Ask the group **where in their body they feel fear, joy, sadness, anger, and disappointment**. Pause between the different emotions to allow the children to connect to the experience. For many children this will not be easy. You could help them by asking whether they feel something in their heads, at the temples, in the heart, the throat, the tummy, on the skin and so on. Not all people feel the same emotion in the same part of the body, but the idea is to create awareness, not expertise.

The children then use the diagram on the activity sheet to indicate the emotions listed.

Tip

There seems to be a connection between specific emotions and the concept of chakras, as John Ruskan explains in his book *Emotional Clearing* (1998).

Timing

5 minutes introduction

4 minutes guided exercise

3 minutes de-roling, summary and conclusion

3 *Where in my body do I feel emotions?*

♟♟♟♟ Large group discussion

Think about the following emotions:

- glad
- sad
- angry
- excited
- scared.

1 Where in your body do you feel these emotions? Write the words glad, sad, angry, excited and scared on the part of the picture below that is the same as where you feel those emotions in your own body.
2 How is your experience different from that of others in your group?

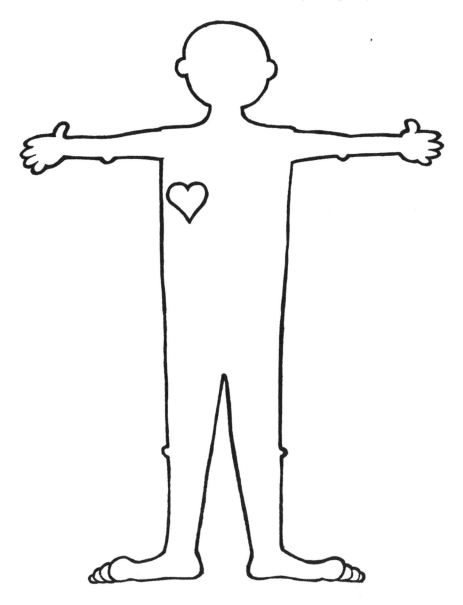

Guidelines: Activity Sheet 4

Dealing with negative emotions

Learning points

This activity expands on Activity Sheet 3. Different emotions affect you differently. It is often when you experience negative or difficult emotions that you don't know what to do or say.

Comments

Tell the group that this activity is related to the previous one. Clarify the meaning of the word 'negative'. It can mean, for example:

- not enjoyable
- not attracting other people
- draining your energy.

Emotions include, for example, anger, hate, jealousy, and loneliness. The result is tiredness, isolation, loneliness and so on.

Instruct the children to sit or lie down in order to be completely comfortable and relaxed. Encourage the group to breathe deeply and relax. Lower your voice and softly, slowly and calmly read through the steps on Activity Sheet 4, allowing time for reflection.

At the end of the activity, tell the children to slowly open their eyes, stretch and get into an upright position.

Ask them how they feel and what were their experiences of the activity. Ask them what they have learnt about themselves from doing the activity.

De-role, that is, come out of the role, by telling the group that the activity is over and that they can let go of the negative emotions.

Thank the group for their co-operation.

Tip

By doing the activity in sequence, the different sensations or experiences are contrasted more effectively.

Timing

5 minutes introduction

4 minutes guided exercise

3 minutes de-roling, summary and conclusion

4 Dealing with negative emotions

👤👤👤👤 Large group discussion

1 What does the word 'negative' mean?

2 Which emotions can be described as 'negative'?

3 What is the result of negative emotions? (What happens to us when we have negative emotions?)

👤👤👤👤 Large group guided exercise

1 Think of a time when you experienced/felt negative emotions.

2 Can you still remember the feeling in your body?

3 Exactly where did you feel it in your body?

4 Describe what you were feeling.

5 Give that feeling a name.

6 What made you feel like that? (What happened?)

7 Why did it make you feel like that? (Should you feel like that?)

8 Would you be comfortable telling others what you are feeling?

9 Did you know whom you could trust and talk to?

10 Would you be able to notice the same feeling in others?

11 Did you know how to act towards the person while they were feeling like that? What would have been best for the other person and yourself?

👤👤👤👤 Large group discussion

What have you learnt from doing this activity?

Guidelines: Activity Sheet 5

Experiencing positive emotions

Learning points

This is an extension of Activity Sheet 4 and addresses a more advanced stage of emotional awareness in which the cause of the emotion is identified. It takes children further in the sense that the issue of trust is considered. One would share emotions with people that one trusts and feels safe with.

Comments

Clarify the meaning of positive emotions. Refer to happiness, excitement, love and so on. List the words on a flipchart or whiteboard. Instruct the children to sit or lie down in order to be completely comfortable and relaxed. Let the group breathe deeply and relax. Talk in a lively voice, and softly and slowly read through the steps, allowing time for reflection.

Ask them how they feel and how they experienced the activity. Ask them what they have learnt about themselves from doing the activity.

Round off the activity by telling the group that it is over and suggesting that they can let go of the emotions if they choose to do so.

Thank the group for their co-operation.

Tip

Background music could be helpful. It is important to create a calm atmosphere and encourage the children to relax.

Timing

5 minutes introduction

2 minutes self-evaluation

3 minutes general discussion

2 minutes summarizing learning points and conclusion

5 Experiencing positive emotions

♟♟♟♟ Large group discussion

1 What does the word 'positive' mean?

2 Which emotions can be described as 'positive'?

3 What is the result of positive emotions? (What happens to us when we have positive emotions?)

♟ Guided exercise

Your teacher will read the following questions out loud, while you simply concentrate. If you find it more comfortable, you may close your eyes. Take a deep breath, sit back and listen to the instructions.

1 Think of a very good time in your life.

2 Can you still remember the feeling in your body?

3 Exactly where did you feel it in your body?

4 Describe what you were feeling.

5 Give that feeling a name.

6 What made you feel like that? (What happened?)

7 Why did it make you feel like that? (Should you feel like that?)

8 Would you have been comfortable to tell others what you were feeling?

9 Who would have been the best people to tell?

10 Have you noticed when another person experienced the same feeling?

11 How did you react towards the other person while they were feeling so good? What would have been the best way of reacting for the other person and yourself?

♟♟♟♟ Large group discussion

What have you learnt from doing this activity?

Guidelines: Activity Sheet 6

Hurry sickness

Learning points

Being irritated and short-tempered can easily become a habit. However, you can do something about your emotions. Impulse control is an important facet of emotional intelligence, and the metaphor of the Pause Button as described by Stephen Covey (1994) is a helpful tool for understanding the concept of emotional control.

This ability to control your emotions or responses (impulse control, emotional control or self-control) is related to the concept of internal locus of control. Essentially you have control over yourself, because it is a choice. When you allow others to upset you, they have control over you and that makes you the victim. Once you become the victim, you may start resenting others when it is in fact your own doing.

Comments

Ask the group about the habit of constantly being in a hurry or being irritated even with little provocation. Reflect on typical situations where people tend to lose their tempers or become irritated; for example, when standing in queues, being stuck in traffic, or holding the line while talking on the telephone.

Instruct the group to do the questionnaire on Activity Sheet 6 on their own. Once it is completed, discuss the questions one by one. Ask the group what they can learn from this activity. Ask them when they think they will next need the skills of calming down and taking control of their feelings.

Tip

Sometimes a person says 'He made me angry', implying that other people have control over our reactions. Ask the children the following question: 'Imagine you are mad at someone, really upset, and you are in the middle of a heated argument. Suppose someone else phones you while you are both arguing. Assume that the person phoning you is someone you admire and respect. How would you respond?' Most people will immediately alter their voice tones, despite being agitated. This is proof of someone's ability to choose their reaction to situations so as to behave appropriately.

Timing

2 minutes introduction

10 minutes sharing in pairs

3 minutes large group discussion and conclusion

6 *Hurry sickness*

🧍 On your own

Some people are quickly irritated and instead of calming down, they react immediately. This habit causes unnecessary stress.

Tick the items in the list below that are true for you.

1 I often get irritated when things don't go my way. ☐

2 I get annoyed when I must wait in a queue. ☐

3 I often feel I haven't done everything I wanted to. ☐

4 I chip in and finish other people's sentences for them when they take too long

   to get to the point. ☐

5 I compare my schoolwork to that of others because I compete with them. ☐

The more items you have marked, the more you might be inclined to become irritated.

👥👥 Large group discussion

● How does it feel when another person becomes irritated and shows their irritation?

● Do irritated people get what they want more easily?

> You can learn to calm down! Learn to use your Pause Button! Next time you feel irritated, do the following to calm down.
>
> ● Breath more slowly.
>
> ● Take a deep breath then, as you breathe out, imagine that you breathe the irritated feelings out to let them vanish in the air.
>
> ● Breathe in deeply and imagine taking in calm blue air.
>
> ● Think of soft light, calm water, beautiful sounds such as the wind blowing softly through the leaves, or gentle waves.
>
> ● Relax your body and open your hands.
>
> ● Say to yourself: I am calm. I control my emotions.
>
> ● Smile.

Remedy for dealing with upsetting emotions

Learning points

You can handle emotions in such a way that you can carry on with your life afterwards.

Comments

Introduce the activity by asking the group whether they have specific strategies or plans to deal with their upsetting emotions. Discuss the list of strategies for each emotion and ask the group to add their ideas.

You may also decide to list the strategies for dealing with happiness and excitement; for example, to share it with somebody you value, or that you know will be interested in the good news.

Timing

5 minutes introduction

6–8 minutes sharing in pairs

2 minutes pairs giving feedback to the larger group

2 minutes verbally summarizing the suggestions of the pairs

7 Remedy for dealing with upsetting emotions

👥 Share in pairs

How would you handle the following emotions?

Anger	Fear
Exercise: run, walk and skip Punch a punching bag Throw balls, stretch, swim Take a few deep breaths Tear newspaper into shreds Listen to music Write your feelings down Squeeze a stress ball or play dough Do a jigsaw puzzle **Your idea?**	Discuss it with someone Name the fear Explain why you have this fear Think: What is the worst thing that can happen? Make sure you tell the right adults about it, such as your parents, carers or a special teacher Can you avoid the fear by starting to do something? **Your idea?**
Sadness	**Aggression**
Cry Talk to a parent or friend Listen to music Write a letter Keep a journal Draw a picture Breathe deeply Exercise Think up a beautiful dream **Your idea?**	Admit that you are a bully Apologize to the person you have hurt Make good by giving something to the person you have hurt Play other games instead of bullying, such as playing with a ball Think of five good things that you know about other people and yourself Take care of a pet **Your idea?**

Adapted from: Leonie Honig (1996)

Guidelines: Activity Sheet 8

Bullies

Learning points

Bullies use aggressive anti-social behaviour to get the attention they need. It is best to deal with them immediately, in public. By acting more self-confidently and reporting bullies immediately, you become less of a soft target. It is important to think ahead and ensure that you are not alone and vulnerable if you notice that you are being targeted. Showing fear and acting timidly, indirectly encourages bullies to try their luck.

Comments

Share in pairs
Instruct the children to complete the first part of Activity Sheet 8 according to their personal experience, responding to the four questions. Each child makes a drawing and explains it to the learning partner.

Small group activity
This could be done as an activity by the small group with feedback to the larger group. Alternatively each small group could first prepare the role play and then perform it in front of the larger group

Large group activity
Discuss within the larger group context the issue of bullying and the effects on others and the community. Consider the possible reasons for bullying and the unfulfilled needs of the bully. Brainstorm possible strategies for dealing effectively with bullying in the school context.

Ask for suggestions in terms of how a school or group could:

- acknowledge the needs of the bully.
- reinforce the behaviour in those who show kindness and empathy.
- support those who stand up for others in need.
- motivate and activate those who show no interest and act with apathy in respect of bullying.

Evaluate the different strategies the groups come up with.

Timing

10–12 minutes share in pairs

15 minutes small group activity (5 minutes preparation, 10 minutes or more taking turns to perform short role plays of 1 to 2 minutes per small group performance – depending on the number of groups)

5 minutes large group activity and conclusion

8 Bullies

👥 Share in pairs

1 How would you describe the behaviours of a bully?

2 Describe the kind of person bullies are most likely to pick on.

3 In the boxes below, draw the face a bully on the left-hand side and the face of the person being bullied on the right-hand side. Discuss the faces with your learning partner.

4 Take turns to describe the emotions you have shown in the faces.

👥👥 Small group activity

In your small group, prepare a role play of a situation during which someone was bullied. First, role play a situation in which the 'victim' makes the wrong moves. Next, perform a role play to show the most effective behaviour on the part of the victim. Be prepared to get feedback and take part in discussions. In the end, you will need to summarize what you have learnt from doing the role plays.

👥👥👥 Large group activity

As a school or a group, how could you:

● deal with bullies.

● praise good, kind behaviour.

● support those who support others and try and protect them.

● encourage those who are merely onlookers to become involved in a project for dealing with bullying.

You might consider handing out badges, certificates, medals and so on.

9 Action plan

The most important thing I have learnt about my emotions is:
When I feel negative, I will …
When I feel angry I will …
When I am scared I will …
When I feel sad I will …
When I feel great I will …
I will think before I act next time when …

Free to be me

I say what I mean

Outline

Outcomes

On completion of this unit, children should be able to stick up for themselves and say how they feel without hurting others.

To be able to do this, children need to:

- understand their own emotions.

- know what caused their emotions.

- say how they feel.

- feel confident expressing their needs.

- choose the right time and place to express their emotions.

- accept that they will not always receive what they ask for.

- be prepared to get feedback and handle it well.

- be sensitive to other people's feelings.

- be comfortable apologizing and asking for forgiveness if they have made a mistake.

- forgive others.

I can be myself and ask for what I want, while I keep other's needs in mind.
I is OK if I have my own needs and things that are important to me apart from what others think I should do.
I can say what I think and feel.
I can make choices although everybody might not feel the same.
It is OK to make mistakes, because no one is perfect.
I can say what I think, while I also listen to what others have to say.

Mindpower (1996)

Overview

Sticking up for myself

When we stick up for ourselves, we are comfortable to let people know what we stand for. It is just as important for people to know what we won't stand for.

To live life fully and enthusiastically, we need a strong belief in ourselves and the self-confidence to act in accordance with what we stand for. Self-esteem and assertiveness are two interdependent attributes. One may well ask whether developing self-esteem will make someone self-assertive, or whether assertive behaviour boosts self-esteem. The point is that resilient people display both attributes.

Assertiveness means that we are comfortable in:

- expressing our emotions and needs
- asking for help
- requesting a change in behaviour if another person's behaviour is out of line
- admiting mistakes
- apologizing for mistakes
- asking for forgiveness
- granting forgiveness.

When we stand up for ourselves and act with self-confidence, it does not mean that we antagonise or provoke people.

Self-esteem

In a world that often makes us feel powerless, one thing we can control is our attitude. Even in the most horrifying circumstances examples of the power of attitude exist: look at Anne Frank, or Helen Keller, or Nelson Mandela, or countless others who refused to accept pity or oblivion as their lot. No one can keep us down without our permission.

Ashton Applewhite (1995)

Self-esteem is the sum of self-confidence and self-respect. It includes:

- feeling good about yourself
- knowing your good points
- being satisfied with yourself
- forgiving yourself
- seeing yourself in positive ways
- doing the best for yourself
- taking risks
- accepting failure
- learning from your mistakes.

Nathaniel Branden (1994) wrote that people with high self-esteem can be knocked down by events, but

Assertive people	Non-assertive people	Aggressive people
• stand up for their rights, needs, desires and beliefs • believe in open, honest expression of their thoughts, without violating the rights of other people • acknowledge basic human rights	• fail to express their feelings, thoughts and beliefs • violate their own human rights • may seem apologetic or self-effacing • may be perceived as weak, lacking in self-esteem	• stand up for their own rights, desires, feelings and beliefs • violate the rights of other people • dominate to get their point across • act as if you are not important
'I win, you win'	**'You win, I lose'**	**'I win, you lose'**

Self-acceptance means that I …	Self-confidence means that I …	Self-esteem means that I …
• appreciate myself • am committed to myself as I am • accept my body, thoughts, actions, emotions and dreams • might disapprove of some aspects of myself • show the compassion of a good friend to myself	• believe in my ability to deal with life • believe in my competence to make choices • plan my life • can satisfy my needs • feel I am worth knowing	• evaluate my mind and my person positively • do not evaluate particular successes or failures or my knowledge or skills • can be very confident of myself yet be uncertain of some of my abilities in specific social situations
Assertiveness means that I …	**Self-respect means that I believe I …**	**Respect for others means that I …**
• express myself • communicate my needs in a straightforward, clear manner without hidden messages or meanings • have positive self-esteem and a good self-image • stand up for myself • am who I am openly • treat myself with respect in all human encounters	• have personal worth • can be happy • am lovable • should be treated with respect • accept that those close to me care about my needs and wants	• show politeness and kindness • see others positively • pay attention to others • care about other's feelings • do not violate other's rights

they overcome setbacks more effectively. Ingredients for developing healthy self-esteem include:

1 Physical safety: to be free from physical harm.
2 Emotional security: the absence of intimidations and fears.
3 Personal identity: to be able to answer the question 'Who am I?'
4 Connection: to experience a sense of belonging and being part of a group.
5 Competence: a sense of feeling capable.
6 Mission: the feeling that one's life has meaning and direction.

Ideally, both the home and the school environments should create the circumstances or 'ingredients' for the development of self-esteem. Self-expression will be more honest and effective in an environment where the ingredients for self-esteem are promoted, protected and fostered.

> Tell me how a person judges his or her self-esteem and I will tell you how that person operates at work, in love, in sex, in parenting, in every important aspect of his existence – and how high he or she is likely to rise. The reputation you have with yourself – your self-esteem – is the single most important factor for a fulfilling life.
>
> *Nathaniel Branden (1994)*

Magicians with words

What causes people to have poor self-esteem and a lack of assertiveness? Sometimes adults (parents and teachers) unknowingly say things that may hurt and lead to self-doubt and poor self-esteem. What people say to someone can have a long-term effect on their life, especially if they see them as experts and therefore take their opinion for the truth! It is said that for every eighteen times the average parent reprimands or criticizes a child, the child is praised, acknowledged or reassured once!

How do comments like these make you feel?

- 'You're crazy!'
- 'You must be stupid to believe that!'
- 'What's going on with you? You're so lazy!'

As opposed to:

- 'When you neglect to hand in your homework, I feel disappointed because you are going to have a lower mark on your report. Can you commit to handing in your assignment next Monday?'

When such an agreement is not honoured, it is appropriate to reprimand, without the parent or teacher losing their temper (and self-esteem)! Nathaniel Branden (1994) wrote: 'Compassion and respect do not imply a lack of firmness.' One can therefore 'draw a line' under it with dignity. The most effective discipline is impersonal yet respectful and caring. When you reprimand someone, be clear on the rules and consequences. Apply rules consistently without exceptions, in a matter of fact manner.

There is a difference between criticism and feedback. Criticism can hurt the character of the person; for example, 'You are lazy!' Feedback is aimed at the behaviour or action and the correction thereof; for example, 'When you neglect to … Can you commit to …?'

Although praise is supposed to be the opposite of criticism, excessive praise might create the impression that 'who I really am is not enough'. That also creates poor self-esteem. The old saying 'Count your words' is still relevant. Don Miguel Ruiz (1952) said:

> Be impeccable with the word. Say only what you mean. Avoid using the word to speak against yourself or to gossip about others. Use the power of the word in the direction of love and truth.

Expressing emotions productively

Next time you express your emotions when giving feedback, you can use the following checklist:

- Do I really want to do this?
- Is this appropriate?
- Is it the right time to do so?
- Is this the place to do it?
- Is it the right thing to do?
- Is this action in line with my value system?
- Will it impact on my integrity and self-esteem?
- Will I respect myself afterwards?
- What will the impact of my decision be?
- Am I willing to deal with the consequences of this action?
- Am I showing respect towards others if I do this?

Guidelines
and
Activity Sheets

The telephone game

Learning points

Misunderstandings happen when we:

- give unclear messages.
- don't ask the right questions to check for understanding.
- do not repeat what the other person has said to ensure that we understand.

Comments

- With the group, discuss the gist of the activity, giving special attention to the rules.
- Instruct the large group to organize themselves in a circle.
- Show the picture below to the child starting the activity.
- When the activity is completed, show the picture to the whole group.
- Work through the questions and list the learning points.

Timing

1 minute introduction

2 minutes explaining rules and organizing group

3 minutes playing the game

3 minutes sharing learning xperiences

1 minute concluding

1 *The telephone game*

👥👥 Large group activity

The whole group sits or stands in a circle. One person (sender) is going to start the game, and the last person (receiver) is going to tell the first person what they have heard.

Rules

1 You have to whisper.

2 You are not allowed to ask any questions.

3 Once you have received the message, you have to pass it on, whether you are sure of the exact words or not.

First person

Look at the picture that your teacher shows you. What do you see? Tell the next person what you see.

Group

Each person passes the message on to the person next to them.

Last person

As you are the last person, you have to tell the others what you have heard.

First person

How is the message different from the one you sent at the start of the game?

👥👥 Large group discussion

How can you ensure that the correct message gets to the receiver?

Guidelines: Activity Sheet 2

Different communication needs

Learning points

Distinguish between:

- **self-talk** – could be unstructured and random.
- **talking to one other person** – depending on the nature of the talk, it will be more formal, informal or relaxed, with opportunity for questions and a quick exchange of information. Body language, word choice and voice tone play a role.
- **talking to a group** – could be formal or informal, with less opportunity to rectify mistakes and for individual questions. Words have to be chosen more carefully, and body language and mannerisms are important.

Comments

The teacher leads the discussion covering the different scenarios and listing learning points.

Tip

Ask for personal experiences, and what the children consider to be the bigger challenge. Share ideas about well-known public speakers. List some of their attributes.

Timing

1 minute introduction

10 minutes answering questions as a large group

3 minutes general discussion and summarizing learning points

1 minute concluding

2 Different communication needs

👥👥 Large group discussion

Explain to each other how 'talking' is different in each situation.

Situation 1

When you sit by yourself and dream or talk to yourself in your head.

Your notes:

Situation 2

When you have a conversation with one other person.

Your notes:

Situation 3

When you make a speech to a large group of people.

Your notes:

Guidelines: Activity Sheet 3

Assess your own self-esteem

Learning points

Self-esteem can be self-developed. By creating the awareness of outward signs and behaviours, we can stimulate the development of self-esteem.

Comments

- Introduce the topic by giving some theoretical background, based on the discussion on public figures and the theory in the overview.
- Instruct the children to work on their own.
- Ensure that there is enough private space for the duration of the self-assessment. Stress the importance of respecting other people's privacy.
- Conclude the activity by asking for general comments.

Tip

Talk about well-known public figures and the perceptions around their self-esteem. Consider how the media play a role in creating perceptions of people.

Timing

2 minutes introduction

5 minutes completing the definition and comparing answers

6 minutes self-assessment

2 minutes concluding

3 Assess your own self-esteem

👤 On your own

What does the word self-esteem mean? Write a definition in the box below.

[ ]

Read through the statements below. Decide whether each one is true or false for you and put a tick in the relevant box. You don't need to share the outcomes of this activity with others, so you can be honest with yourself. This is for your eyes only.

Statement	True	False
1 I can easily admit a mistake.	☐	☐
2 I can easily talk to people that I meet for the first time.	☐	☐
3 I do what I know is right, even if others don't agree.	☐	☐
4 I am comfortable when someone compliments me.	☐	☐
5 I congratulate others when they achieve success.	☐	☐
6 I don't compare myself to others.	☐	☐
7 I accept people who have different needs.	☐	☐
8 I can tell other people that I love them.	☐	☐
9 I love myself and accept myself as much as I love and accept others.	☐	☐
10 I am comfortable with myself when I am alone.	☐	☐

The more ticks you have under 'True' the higher your self-esteem is. If your self-esteem is not as high as you would like it to be, don't be disheartened, self-esteem is something you can develop. Completing these activity sheets could help you to develop your self-esteem.

Guidelines: Activity Sheet 4

I can say no, nicely

Learning points

Assertiveness means calmly and consistently standing up for our rights, without losing our temper or giving up our rights.

Comments

Option one

Perform this activity as a role play in which selected children play out the scene in front of the whole group so that the group can learn from it and make comments. Brief the role players beforehand and supply a pen, 'hamburger' and sheet of paper for a more convincing act. Three different teams could each play a scene.

Option two

The children work in groups of four to perform their own role play. Tell the children that they need to give each group member a number from one to four. Call each 'number' group to one side and give them the following instructions: number '1's should be very self-assured, stubborn and even rude when they play the role of the borrower, seller and inactive group member; number '2's should be very shy and sorry for themselves when they represent the submissive person; number '3's should be aggressive, talk loudly, be threatening and intimidating; number '4's need to be briefed on assertiveness – they need to insist calmly on getting the pen replaced, the money back for the hamburger, and the portion of the team member's work.

Conclusion

Once the role plays are completed, summarize the learning points and conclude with a list of important points to remember when confronting another person.

Timing

2 minutes introduction

5 minutes discussing the role plays, organizing groups and players

12 minutes performing role plays

4 minutes discussing the learning points

2 minutes concluding

4 *I can say no, nicely*

👥👥👥 Small group role play

Pretend that the following situations happen at your school. How would you handle them?

Situation 1

A classmate borrows your favourite pen during an exam, because he has lost his pen during break time. When he gives it back to you, the tip is damaged and you cannot use it anymore.

Situation 2

During break time, somebody sells hamburgers on your school's playground. You did not have breakfast this morning, and you did not bring anything to eat. You have very little pocket money left, but you are so hungry that you decide to buy a hamburger. As you bite into the hamburger, you discover that it is completely dried out and mouldy – not edible at all. With no money left, and you still being very hungry, you decide to go back to the person selling the hamburgers and ask for your money back.

Situation 3

Four of you have to complete an assignment before the end of next week. Three of you work very hard on the assignment, but one member of the group has not done anything yet, and keeps on making excuses. You need to address the person who does not contribute.

Performing the role play

Give each person in your group a number from one to four. For all three role plays:

- **player one** will be the person who borrows the pen, sells the hamburgers and does not do his part of the assignment.

- **player two** will be a submissive (shy) person.

- **player three** will be an aggressive (very angry) person.

- **player four** will be an assertive (calm and persistent) person.

Once you have completed the role play, you have to:

- explain how your role made you feel.

- decide which approach (assertive, aggressive, submissive) is most successful.

Guidelines: Activity Sheet 5

Check your body language

Learning points

Body language is something we could be unaware of, and could either be appropriate or distracting. By sharing the activity, we can learn about ourselves and act on the information. This activity expands on the Johari window concept of how we form our self-concept based on a combination of our own and others' viewpoints. It stimulates self-reflection and promotes tactful feedback.

Comments

- Read though the list of behaviours and clarify any uncertainties.
- Ask everybody to start at the same time.
- Give a time limit beforehand.
- After 5 minutes of self-assessment, instruct the children to exchange books and assess each other.

Conclude the activity by asking a general question of the group, such as 'What was interesting or helpful about the exercise?' Refer to the Johari window concept, and the value of getting honest, tactful feedback.

Tip

Emphasize the importance of tactful feedback and honesty.

Timing

2 minutes introduction
5 minutes self-assessment
5 minutes assessing each other
5 minutes general discussion
1 minute concluding

5 *Check your body language*

👥 **Share in pairs**

● Work with a learning partner.

● Tick the statements you
  believe are **true** for you
  in the column
  headed '✔'.

● Swop activity sheets with
  your learning partner and put
  a cross next to the statements
  you think are **true** for your
  learning partner in the
  column headed '✗'

● Compare the results and
  share your learning points
  with each other.

		✔	✗			✔	✗
1	Look directly at the other person's eyes when talking			14	Keep your hands on your hips		
2	Blink rapidly			15	Keep your eyes downcast		
3	Have an open facial expression			16	Use a firm voice		
4	Stay balanced when you stand			17	Laugh at the wrong time		
5	Bite lips			18	Stare into the distance		
6	Stay relaxed			19	Clear your throat too often		
7	Use your hands to gesture			20	Speak rapidly		
8	Look bored			21	Speak softly		
9	Wrinkle your forehead			22	Speak too much		
10	Close your lips tightly			23	Speak too little		
11	Clench your teeth			24	Fiddle with jewellery or hands		
12	Speak loudly			25	Point fingers		
13	Nod too much			26	Wet your lips all the time		

Adapted from Louise Welsh Schrank (1991)

Guidelines: Activity Sheet 6

Feedback rules

Learning points

Blaming, shaming and naming are not good feedback practices because they break rather than build self-esteem and relationships.

Comments

General discussion with attention to the questions.

Tip

Discuss embarrassing times when other people's rude remarks elicited negative reactions from you or someone else.

Timing

1 minute introduction

5 minutes general discussion and sharing of personal experiences

3 minutes learning points and offering alternatives

1 minute concluding

6 Feedback rules

👥 Large group work

When you say how you feel (give feedback), it is often best to avoid the following:

- name calling (Lazy-bones, Liar! Thief!).
- blaming the other person (It's your fault!).

You did it on purpose ...

Bully!

It's your fault!

You don't care!

You are stupid!

You are irresponsible!

👥 Large group discussion

How does it make a person feel when they are told something such as:

You are **slow**!	You are **cheeky**!
You are **naughty**!	You are **impossible**!
You are **disruptive**!	You are a pain in the **neck**!
You are always **late**!	You are **stupid**!
You are **rude**!	You are an **idiot**!

Guidelines: Activity Sheet 7

A recipe for proper feedback

Learning points

There is a difference between criticism and feedback, and when we have a recipe for feedback, we can refine the skill. It is not easy to give negative feedback but it can really help another person, apart from being a tactful way of expressing our needs and emotions.

Comments

Begin by providing a few general examples (see Guidelines pages 107–108).

- Ask the children to work in pairs or small groups to complete the activity sheet examples on pages 110–111.
- To finish, the pairs or small groups take turns to share their efforts with the large group.
- Allow comments or additional inputs.

Tips

- Do several examples to introduce the concept (see Guidelines pages 107–108).
- During feedback, ensure that you guide and support, rather than correct.

Timing

2 minutes introduction

5 minutes clarifying the format of the example for giving feedback

10 minutes for practical work – sharing in pairs works well – each pair gets one situation to work on

15 minutes for large group sharing of each pair's answers and discussing alternatives

2 minutes concluding

What do you say

Examples are guidelines, there could be many more alternatives.

Your friend borrows something and does not give it back	
Describe what the person did	When you borrow something from me and do not return it
Describe how you feel	I feel frustrated
Tell the person what the result is	because I cannot do my work without it.
Ask the person to do something else	Can you please give it back now?

Your best friend talks about you behind your back	
Describe what the person did	When I hear that you say things behind my back
Describe how you feel	I feel disappointed/hurt/sad
Tell the person what the result is	because I don't know what is going on.
Ask the person to do something else	Can you rather tell me what is bothering you so that we can talk things over?

Someone bullies one of your classmates	
Describe what the person did	When you hurt Joe
Describe how you feel	I feel angry/ashamed
Tell the person what the result is	because it makes him feel uncomfortable/lonely/left out. OR because it makes you look bad.
Ask the person to do something else	Could you please play with someone else instead of bothering him?

Your mother arrives late to pick you up from school	
Describe what the person did	Mum, when you arrive late to pick me up
Describe how you feel	I get worried/frustrated
Tell the person what the result is	because I don't know what is going on/I am tired/I battle to finish my homework/chores.
Ask the person to do something else	Can you please be here on time?

The lady behind the counter ignores you when you want to pay for a present for a friend

Describe what the person did	When you don't attend to me
Describe how you feel	I feel frustrated/ignored/uneasy
Tell the person what the result is	because I cannot finish my shopping in time.
Ask the person to do something else	Could you please indicate that you notice me and help me when it is my turn?

Somebody teases you about your clothes

Describe what the person did	When you make remarks about my clothes/something personal
Describe how you feel	I feel humiliated/sad
Tell the person what the result is	because others laugh at me.
Ask the person to do something else	Could you please keep your remarks to yourself? Could you please mind your own business?

Your best friend ignores you and spends break time with somebody else

Describe what the person did	When you don't talk to me
Describe how you feel	I feel hurt/sad/excluded
Tell the person what the result is	because I don't know why you are ignoring me.
Ask the person to do something else	Can we talk it over?/Can you tell me whether something is bothering you?

Somebody removes a book from your room without asking your permission

Describe what the person did	When you take a book from my room
Describe how you feel	I feel irritated/annoyed
Tell the person what the result it	because I spend a long time looking for it/cannot finish my reading.
Ask the person to do something else	Can you ask permission/let me know next time you want to borrow it?

7 A recipe for proper feedback

👤 Theory

'WIN message' is a short name for the manner in which **feedback** should be given. It **focuses on the behaviour** and **not on the person**. It also describes behaviour and not the intention.

W stands for **When**, and describes a specific behaviour or action.

I stands for **'I'-messages** and explains **how the sender feels**.

N stands for the **negative results** of the **behaviour**.

Formulate WIN messages

W I N

When you ... arrive late for drama class

(Explain what is happening)

I feel frustrated

(Say how you feel)

because the whole group has to wait and we do not get the work done.

(Describe the negative results of the other person's actions)

Feedback on negative behaviour

	Example
Describe what the person did	*When you do not arrive on time*
Describe how you feel	*I am annoyed/I get nervous*
Tell the person what the result is	*because the whole group has to wait and we waste time*
Ask the person to do something else	*Would it be possible to be on time from now on? Can you commit to that?*

👤👤👤👤 Large group discussion

'What is the difference between criticism and feedback on negative behaviour?

7 A recipe for proper feedback (continued)

What do you say

Your friend borrows something and does not give it back	
Describe what the person did	
Describe how you feel	
Tell the person what the result is	
Ask the person to do something else	

Your best friend talks about you behind your back	
Describe what the person did	
Describe how you feel	
Tell the person what the result is	
Ask the person to do something else	

Someone bullies one of your classmates	
Describe what the person did	
Describe how you feel	
Tell the person what the result is	
Ask the person to do something else	

Your mother arrives late to pick you up from school	
Describe what the person did	
Describe how you feel	
Tell the person what the result is	
Ask the person to do something else	

Unit 4   Free to be me

7 A recipe for proper feedback (continued)

The lady behind the counter ignores you when you want to pay for a present for a friend	
Describe what the person did	
Describe how you feel	
Tell the person what the result is	
Ask the person to do something else	

Somebody teases you about your clothes	
Describe what the person did	
Describe how you feel	
Tell the person what the result is	
Ask the person to do something else	

Your best friend ignores you and spends break time with somebody else	
Describe what the person did	
Describe how you feel	
Tell the person what the result is	
Ask the person to do something else	

Somebody removes a book from your room without asking your permission	
Describe what the person did	
Describe how you feel	
Tell the person what the result it	
Ask the person to do something else	

Guidelines: Activity Sheet 8

Strokes and positive feedback

Learning points

When we hear the word stroke, we may think of a game, such as golf, or painting in which we use a brush stroke, or an illness and so on. However, for this activity a stroke is something else. Imagine gently stroking a cat or dog. What is the reaction of the animal? Or, imagine you feel down and a friend touches your arm to console you. How does it feel? Or, imagine getting a nice present from someone.

Giving positive strokes or feedback builds relationships. It requires good self-esteem to acknowledge other's strong points. It represents a positive outlook and supports friendships.

Through positive strokes you build an 'emotional bank account' or reservoir of good feelings towards yourself. You endear yourself to others when you give them heartfelt compliments of positive feedback.

Comments

- Discuss the theory in a general, large group discussion, with inputs from the group.
- Ask the group to offer more examples of strokes.

Timing

2 minutes introduction

8 minutes large group discussion

2 minutes concluding

8 Strokes and positive feedback

👥 Share in pairs

A positive or good stroke is something enjoyable that one person gives another person. A compliment is a stroke. Telling someone what you appreciate about them is a stroke. A stroke is the same as positive feedback – acknowledging something that you appreciate about another person.

What other examples can you think of?

Think of the people you appreciate and that make your life worthwhile. How can you let them know that you value them?

👥👥 Large group work

1 Give a few more examples of positive feedback.

2 Why do we give positive feedback?

3 How does it make you feel when you get positive feedback?

Guidelines: Activity Sheet 9

Apologize for mistakes

Learning points

When we do something that is hurtful to another person and we want to make up for it, we need to say that we are sorry and ask the person to forgive us. For most of us it is difficult to admit that we made a mistake. We also do not know whether the person is going to forgive us and accept the apology. But, regardless of how the other person is going to behave, we have to do the right thing. We can't expect forgiveness, because forgiveness is a gift. If we don't feel sorry, we shouldn't say that we are sorry. When we apologize, we also make a commitment not to do the same thing again.

Love is the medicine for hurt and anger. To find love, we have to forgive. When we forgive, the resentment goes away.

> The highest wisdom is kindness.
>
> *The Talmud (fourth century)*

Comments

- Talk about the principles of making mistakes, regretting them and apologizing.
- Ask the children 'What makes apologizing so difficult?'
- Talk about the requirements for making apologies.

Tip

Discuss examples of well-known public figures and their mistakes, how it was handled, and what the right/best alternative would be.

Timing

2 minutes general introduction

5 minutes large group discussion

5 minutes sharing personal experiences and trying out the formula using real-life examples

3 minutes concluding and discussing home play

9 Apologize for mistakes

👤 Theory

Read the following recipe for forgiveness.

1 Admit to yourselves that you made a mistake.

2 Admit to the other person that you made a mistake.

3 Say that you are sorry.

4 Try and understand how you made the other person feel.

5 Admit that it was wrong.

6 Ask for forgiveness.

7 Don't make the same mistake again.

The other person can:

● listen to your apology.

● forgive you.

● postpone forgiving you until they see whether you will make the same mistake again.

● decide not to forgive you.

To receive forgiveness is A GIFT.

It cannot be demanded.

It cannot always be granted.

👤 On your own

1 When you go home today, your challenge is to give feedback on positive behaviour to every person in your household during the coming week.

2 Also give proper feedback on negative behaviour when necessary.

3 Be prepared to share your experiences with the group during the next session.

Guidelines: Activity Sheet 10

Group play

Learning points

It is a life skill to be positively oriented and notice the good points in others. It signifies a person with grace and kindness. It builds friendships and trust.

Comments

Arrange the children into small groups and read through the following instructions which appear on Activity Sheet 10.

1 Write your name in the space at the top.
2 Pass your activity sheet to the person on your right.
3 Accept the activity sheet from the person on your left.
4 Write down what you admire or like about the person whose name is at the top and sign your name.
5 Once you have completed the positive feedback, pass the activity sheet to the person on your right.
6 Repeat the process until you receive your own activity sheet.

Tip

Emphasize the importance of tact, good manners, kindness and respect.

Timing

1 minute introduction

2 minutes explaining the purpose and rules of the game

20–25 minutes passing paper around

2 minutes concluding

Personal Skills for Effective Learning

10 *Group play*

⛉ Small group activity

Instructions

1 Write your name in the space at the top of the box (below).

2 Pass your activity sheet to the person on your right

3 Accept the activity sheet from the person on your left.

4 Write down what you admire or like about the person whose name is at the top and sign your name.

5 Once you have completed the positive feedback, pass the activity sheet to the person on your right.

6 Repeat the process until you receive your own activity sheet.

Name

11 Action plan

In future I would like to make sure that I ...	
Speak more clearly	☐
Choose my words carefully	☐
Check my body language	☐
Think of others' needs and feelings before I act	☐
Give feedback in the right place and time	☐
Build my self-confidence	☐
Act assertively (stand up for myself)	☐
Apologize when necessary	☐
Forgive others	☐
Give positive strokes	☐
Give feedback on unacceptable behaviour	☐
Ask for strokes when I need encouragement	☐

My world

I have my own identity

Outline

Outcomes

On completion of this unit, children should understand what sets them apart from others and what makes them fit in with others. To be able to do that, children should be able to:

- name the things that make them different.

- tell others what is typical of their country, their culture, their family and themselves.

- know some facts about other cultures.

- be able to 'stand in another person's shoes' for better understanding.

- list what all people want.

- describe how they and others should behave to contribute to good relationships and support each other.

> The golden rule should be revised to read:
> Do not do unto others as you would they should do unto you.
> Their tastes may not be the same.
>
> *George Bernard Shaw*

> Life is like an echo. What you send out returns to you.
> What you give, you get.
>
> *Anon*

Overview

Personal universe

In the normal course of events, we do not listen to discover what the other person's reality is. We only listen to evaluate the rightness or wrongness of the other person's reality compared to our own.

Stewart Emery (as quoted in IBM, 1994)

Each of us looks at life from a personal viewpoint. From this egocentric or ethnocentric point of view, we are at the middle of our universe and other people and events revolve around us. We tend to assume that the way we see things is the way things should be.

In reality, the world is polycentric. There are as many midpoints as there are people to look out from them. Our challenge is to blend our viewpoints into a common understanding through a tolerant attitude and a real interest in other people's realities.

During the early stage of adolescence, ages ten to twelve, children ask themselves 'Who am I?' In the search for their own identity, children separate themselves emotionally from their parents and even challenge their parents' norms. Despite this separation, they still need parental love, acceptance, nurturing and support.

On the other hand, during this stage children form closer bonds with peers and have a deep need for group acceptance. Their emotional experiences may be contradictory and complex, with a combination of emotional outbursts and feelings of vulnerability occurring at the same time. They fear the pain of rejection and ridicule and follow trends very carefully.

Common fears include the following:

From a distance some children are so similar in appearance that it is sometimes difficult to identify a particular child in a group! This awareness of personal identity versus group conformity relates directly to the issue of diversity.

What is culture?

Cultural diversity includes 'racial diversity', but in reality we could be of the same race and, based on personality differences or other factors, find it impossible to see eye to eye.

Culture is: habits… upbringing… sex… education… nationality… organization… dress… food… rituals… experience… caste… social status… career… size of family… birth order… time you were born… values… norms… television… gestures… music… language rules… poetry… role of father… literature… role of mother… role of first child… money economy… school system… research… advertising… attitude to technology… radio… media… newspaper… expression of feelings… censorship… expression of thought… intolerance…

So, eye contact can show confidence…or lack of respect. Avoiding eye contact can show respect…or indicate guilt. Slurping soup can show appreciation…or bad table manners. Being late can show thoughtlessness …or thoughtfulness. Giving a hug can show friendliness…or rudeness. Smiling can mean yes…or no.

Working Smarter: The Learner Within (IBM, 1994)

Ridiculed	To be laughed at, made fun of, not be taken seriously.
Ignored (not acknowledged)	To be forgotten, abandoned, unimportant, invisible, non-existent, excluded.
Judged	Made to feel guilty, ostracized, shamed, disapproved, devalued.
Manipulated	To be dominated, controlled, used, smothered.

What makes people different?

Genetic blueprint

No two people (even identical twins) have the same genes. Biology determines our gender, colour of skin, hair and eyes, physical characteristics such as height and sometimes even a disability or dysfunction such as a shorter limb or colour blindness. Some families are known for outsanding athletic capabilities, musicality and so on.

Race

This influences the characteristics of a person who comes from a common genetic pool and could determine physical and other attributes.

Gender

Proper behaviour and role expectations are often based on cultural premises. We are taught what is expected from us, being male or female.

Family

Families create their own unique cultures. Family rules determine acceptable behaviours and attitudes, and support customs and rituals.

Generation

Different generations were exposed to different world realities. A person born during the early part of the previous century would have a very different frame of reference from a person of a later generation born nearer the end of the century.

Immediate environment

Schools cultivate their own cultures through rules and rituals or traditions. Each school is known for an outstanding characteristic that sets it apart from other schools.

Past conditioning

The homes, schools and communities where we grow up have an influence on our perceptions and outlook on life. What we have heard others say or what we have observed others doing could become our measurement for appropriateness.

Habits

Aristotle said that we are what we repeatedly do. Excellence, then, is not an act but a habit. While many habits are based on sound thinking and/or principles, we also form habits out of necessity, for survival, or even for convenience.

Frame of reference

Our frame of reference plays an important role in our viewpoint and outlook on life. A well-travelled person, for instance, might have a different outlook on international issues to a person who does not watch the news or read contemporary information.

Religion

Religion is possibly one of the most sensitive discussion points one could introduce into a conversation; at the same time, it is often viewed as the basis for some of the fiercest wars in history.

Politics

The strong reactions some people display when confronted with political issues are testimony to the impact political viewpoints can have on people. While many people try to avoid political issues, others are intrigued by politics.

Financial status

The division between rich and poor is still very strong. The 'haves' and the 'have nots' live in different realities.

Region

The activities of the region we grow up in establish a framework of what life and making a living is about.

Rich traditions set regions apart from each other and could be a source of pride for the inhabitants. When people reflect on the places where they were born and bred, it is often with passion and vivid memory.

Geography

The life style in colder countries is very different from that in hot countries. Seasons in the northern and southern hemisphere are the opposite during the year. Variations in weather patterns, economic activities and links with the outside world make countries different.

Personality

In work and private life, people with different personalities may find it difficult to understand each other and work together. The same differences can, however, form the basis of dynamic teams.

Defining some diversity-related terminology

Discrimination means to make a distinction. It can also mean that you treat a person differently, or as an inferior.

Prejudice refers to adverse judgements or opinions formed without factual verification and based on assumptions.

Racism is the belief that human races have distinctive characteristics that make some races superior with the right to rule over other races.

Sexism is based on the assumption that one sex is superior and therefore has the right to define the other sex's role in society.

Stereotypes is a way of categorizing people of a certain gender, race, religion, career or such like as being exactly the same.

Resilience is enhanced when we are able to break free from the limiting elements of stereotypes and other forms of cultural biases and focus on the positives.

Finding common ground

In the normal course of events, we do not listen to discover what the other person's reality is. We only listen to evaluate the rightness or wrongness of the other person's reality compared to our own.

Stewart Emery (as quoted in IBM, 1994)

We can see diversity as a problem or as an opportunity. The choice is ours. Difference is the source of innovation, because people with unusual viewpoints have fresh ideas and see new possibilities. When we are open to other standpoints and realities, we open the possibilities for finding common understanding.

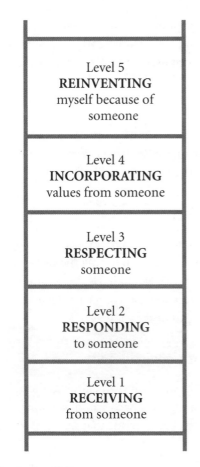

Level 5
REINVENTING
myself because of someone

Level 4
INCORPORATING
values from someone

Level 3
RESPECTING
someone

Level 2
RESPONDING
to someone

Level 1
RECEIVING
from someone

Stages of relationships

Working Smarter: The Learner Within (IBM, 1994)

This diagram explains that we can learn from others without giving up our own identity. On a personal level, we can learn from others to improve ourselves. We can also take the best out of other cultures, learn from them, incorporate them into our own culture and thereby improve what we have. Learning implies a change in behaviour – we cannot convince others that we have learnt something if they cannot notice any changes in us.

If we focus on what everybody needs (universal needs) instead of emphasizing what we do not agree on, we may find common ground. All people want safety, love, health, happiness, peace, good relationships and so on. To fulfil those needs, we need to work together. Qualities that inspire us, such as peace and beauty, spring from diversity – a rainbow is more beautiful than a single colour and a chorus moves us with the harmony of different voices.

Profound changes in our world are forcing people to break free from cultural prohibitions that have suppressed the development of their inner strengths. Psychological health, like physical health, must be self-developed and I see many signs that it is increasing.

Al Siebert (1996)

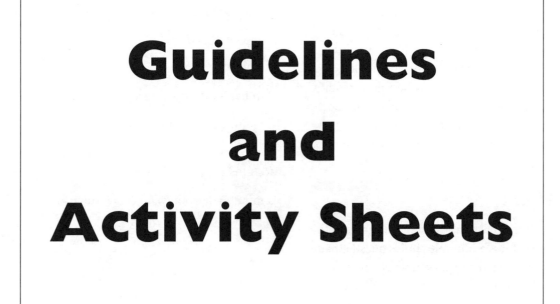

Guidelines
and
Activity Sheets

The game of life

Learning points

This is an experiential activity to stimulate empathy with others who live in different circumstances. The idea is to reflect on the aspects outside our control and those things we can change. For example, we cannot change our date of birth, what we look like and so on. Even though we may be able to modify some things about ourselves (we can change our looks, gender, current environment at a price), in essence there are many things beyond our control.

Comments

- The children mark the different numbers in the matrix as if it is a multiple choice questionnaire.
- Only when the matrix is completed are they allowed to turn to the legend. They then transfer the answers from the legend to the outcomes table on the activity sheet.
- The children introduce their new identities to the smaller group, discuss the consequences of being somebody else and then report back to the larger group.
- Lead the larger group discussion.
- Encourage appreciation for differences and acceptance of personal circumstances.

Tip

You could use pictures of people from different countries and put them on display. Play music typical of different cultures. Ask the children to link the picture or music to its countries or regions of origin.

Timing:

2 minutes introduction and explaining rules

10 minutes individual activity

5 minutes general large group discussion of how it feels to have a new identity

3 minutes de-roling and concluding

1 *The game of life*

On your own

This activity sheet is completed in the same way as a multiple choice questionnaire. Use the matrix below and circle one number in each row from A to J.

A	1	2	3	4	5
B	6	7	8	9	10
C	11	12	13	14	15
D	16	17	18	19	20
E	21	22	23	24	25
F	26	27	28	29	30
G	31	32	33	34	35
H	36	37	38	39	40
I	41	42	43	44	45
J	46	47	48	49	50

1 Go to the next page and match the numbers with the items.

2 Transfer (write) the outcomes to the spaces below.

A	
B	
C	
D	
E	
F	
G	
H	
I	
J	

Small group activity/ Large group activity

Introduce the new you to the group!

Discuss how this new identity makes you feel.

1 *The game of life: legend*

A = Age

1 = 15–20 years   2 = 20–30 years
3 = 30–40 years   4 = 40–50 years
5 = older than 50 years

B = Health

6 = Terminally ill   7 = HIV positive
8 = Healthy but unfit   9 = Healthy but blind
10 = Excellent health and fit

C = Physical

11 = Very short and overweight   12 = Medium height with ideal weight
13 = Overweight quadriplegic   14 = Very thin, tall and blind
15 = Very tall and overweight with a hearing problem

D = Gender

16 = Male   17 = Female
18 = Male   19 = Female
20 = Choose

E = Nationality

21 = American   22 = Japanese
23 = Iraqi   24 = British
25 = Zimbabwean

1 *The game of life: legend* (continued)

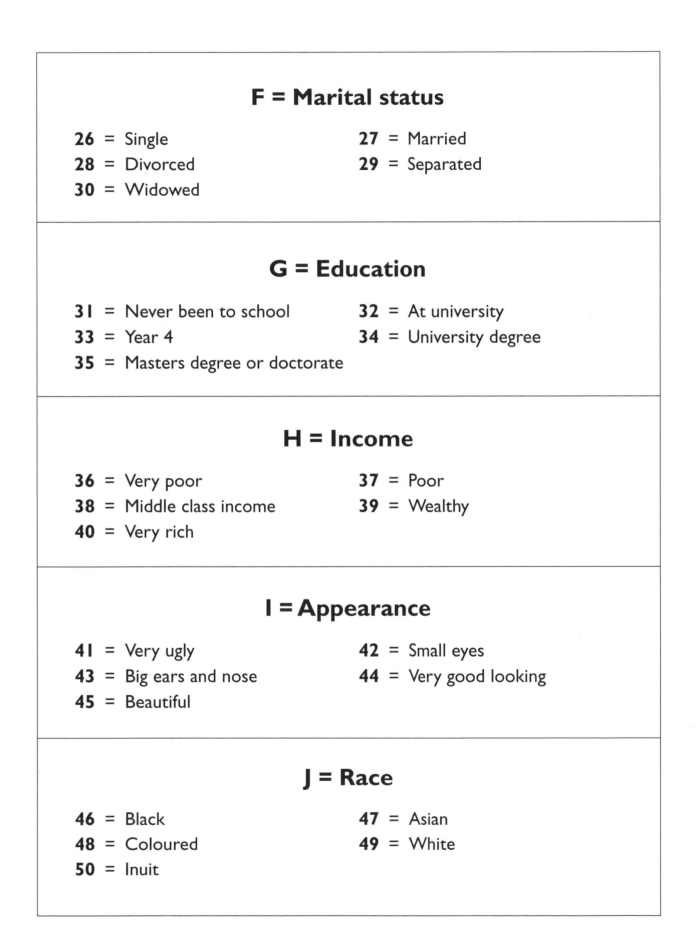

F = Marital status

26 = Single   **27** = Married
28 = Divorced   **29** = Separated
30 = Widowed

G = Education

31 = Never been to school   **32** = At university
33 = Year 4   **34** = University degree
35 = Masters degree or doctorate

H = Income

36 = Very poor   **37** = Poor
38 = Middle class income   **39** = Wealthy
40 = Very rich

I = Appearance

41 = Very ugly   **42** = Small eyes
43 = Big ears and nose   **44** = Very good looking
45 = Beautiful

J = Race

46 = Black   **47** = Asian
48 = Coloured   **49** = White
50 = Inuit

Guidelines: Activity Sheet 2

My frame of reference

Learning points

This activity promotes self-awareness as well as an awareness of what makes us unique and how others need acknowledgement of the things they care about.

This activity aims to challenge stereotypes and discrimination.

Comments

- Read through all the questions, clarify uncertainties and then allow the sharing of information in groups of four or five.
- Groups should be as diverse as possible with a mix of races, cultures, genders and so on.
- The sharing of information creates a deeper understanding of other people's values, preferences and challenges.
- Work to ensure an atmosphere of mutual respect.
- Towards the end of the session, bring everyone together as a large group to give feedback to each other.

Timing

2 minutes overview

3 minutes small group discussion of first activity

2 minutes large group feedback from small groups

12 minutes small group discussion

5 minutes feedback

3 minutes summarizing

2 minutes concluding

2 My frame of reference

This activity sheet is a tool to help you think about the many ways in which we are different, as well as the ways in which we are similar. It is done in the form of a small group discussion, and if you could form a group of people who are very different from each other, coming from different cultures, it is more interesting. Be prepared to give feedback to the large group once you have completed your discussion.

👥 Small group discussion 1
My physical appearance and personality

Pretend that you are talking to a stranger over the telephone. You have to meet the person somewhere.

1 How do you describe yourself to the stranger?
2 How would others, who know you well, describe you?

👥 Small group discussion 2

Complete the following phrases.

Gender

Girls are ...
Boys are ...
I am ...
A real man should be ...
A real woman should be ...

Family

Our family consists of (who are the family members) ...
My place in our family is (are you the only child, the eldest and so on) ...
Children should be ...
One thing my parents are very strict about is ...
A special occasion in our family is ...
Our favourite food is ...
For some people, Christmas is a special event. Where I come from, a special event is ...

Age

When children talk to older people, such as their grandparents or older relatives, they have to ...
Where I come from, people show respect for their parents and grandparents by ...

Stereotypes

The best job is ...
Doctors are ...
Rich people are ...
People from the UK are ...

Teachers are ...
Children are ...
Americans are ...

Nationality

In my household, we consider people from other countries as ...
People from other race groups are ...

Guidelines: Activity Sheet 3

What is acceptable?

Learning points

Although certain expressions, styles, trends and mannerisms can be fashionable at a certain point in time, good manners are more universal and long term. Respect is not about impressing others, but rather about building good relationships.

Comments

- Guide the group interaction by reading through points 1–5 on Activity Sheet 3 and clarifying uncertainties before the children start to respond to the points and the topics they cover.
- Split the group into boys and girls. Invite each group to appoint a scribe.
- Give each group a sheet of paper and thick pens to write with. Instruct the groups to record their findings on the paper. They need to ensure that the size of the writing is suitable for a large group discussion at the end of the activity.

Tip

Boys and girls should ideally be split into separate teams to add some fun and to create a kind of 'competition' between the genders for interest's sake. At the end of the activity, find the elements that are true for both genders and which could possibly relate to good manners, irrespective of gender.

Timing

3 minutes introduction and organizing groups

15 minutes group work

15 minutes feedback to the larger group

2 minutes summarizing and concluding

3 What is acceptable?

ⵊⵊⵊⵊ Large group activity

If possible, girls and boys should work in separate teams for this activity. Ideas or opinions are written on sheets of paper that you are going to put up and discuss in front of the whole group.

Think of individuals of the opposite gender and describe what you find pleasing/not nice regarding the following:

1   **How a person dresses**
    The neatness of a person's clothes and their style of dressing.

2   **Personal habits**
    General habits like being clean, or mannerisms such as the way a person yawns, sneezes and so on.

3   **Manner of speaking**
    How a person pronounces words, the types of words a person uses, how loud or soft a person talks and so on.

4   **Self-confidence**
    Some people are shy, others are overconfident and some just have funny habits of sitting and standing. It is possible that some people come across as trying to impress others.

5   **How a person deals with others**
    The way in which a person talks to others, what a person says about others, how a person treats others, how a person deals with people from the opposite gender.

Discuss within the group, what is the difference between:

● my own taste
● what is 'in' at the moment (fashionable)
● good manners that are accepted in most places.

Guidelines: Activity Sheet 4

What makes people different?

Learning points

This activity aims to help children think about the different aspects of cultural diversity. It serves as a summary of learning points from all the previous exercises in this unit.

Comments

- This could either be a whole-group discussion, with a scribe making notes on a flipchart or board; or it could be a small-group exercise followed by feedback to the larger group.
- Start off the activity by giving two or three examples of what is expected. This would mean listing on the board a few words of what makes us different.

Tip

A quick revision of the outcomes of the previous activity sheets on diversity could serve as a warm-up exercise.

Timing

1 minute giving instructions

10 minutes group work or compiling the list as a large group

1 minute summarizing

4 *What makes people different?*

👥 Small group activity

In groups of four or five, make a list of all the things you can think of that make people different. Your challenge is to list as many things as possible.

On the list, tick the things one can change. For example:

● Can you change your date of birth?

● Can you change your race group?

● Can you change your level of education?

Consider how it makes you feel that you cannot change certain things.

How does it make you feel when you think about others and their circumstances?

Guidelines: Activity Sheet 5

Standing in someone else's shoes

Learning points

By imagining yourself as a member of the opposite sex and by acting like a person from the opposite sex, you learn to acknowledge the other person's reality. The same principle applies to people from another country, race and so on. If you can imagine the life of another person, harmful stereotyping, racism, and bias can be avoided.

Comments

- For the period of the lesson (or school day if possible), the whole group has to switch roles. Playing different games during break, standing differently, talking differently. In essence this should be a light-hearted activity.
- At the end of the activity, ask the children what their experiences were and what they enjoyed or disliked about the roles. If they have made drawings about aspects of the life of the opposite gender that they found interesting, this could be incorporated in the discussion.
- De-roling, that is shedding their role, is essential at the end.
- Thank the children for their participation in this challenging activity.

Timing

3 minutes briefing, setting boundaries, determining ground rules

15 minutes de-roling and discussing learning points at the end of the day

5 *Standing in someone else's shoes*

👥 Small group activity

For this activity imagine that you are a member of the opposite gender. You have to talk, walk and act like one would expect a member of that gender would do.

At the end of the period, each group has to write down on a sheet of paper all the positive and negative things about being male or female. Groups can take turns to present their comments to the larger group.

You may make a drawing of something about the life of a person of the opposite gender that interests you and that you do not mind sharing with the group.

Guidelines: Activity Sheet 6

All people need ...

Learning points

The aim of this activity is to help the children focus on things we all value. Common needs such as the need to be happy, to be loved, to have relationships with others, health, opportunities for growth, enjoyment, fun, safety and so on.

Comments

- Hand out sheets of paper with coloured markers (felt tip pens) for small group work. The children could use the activity sheet if preferred.
- Groups work on their own and have to list a few universal needs. They then draw a design or logo representing the common need that their group consider to be most important.
- At the end of the activity, groups have to give feedback to the larger group, and explain their choice of logo.
- Wrap up the exercise by summarizing what was brought up.

Timing

2 minutes briefing

15–20 minutes designing the logo

15 minutes presentation to the group

6 *All people need*

👥 **Small group activity**

Complete the phrase: 'All people need...'

With a partner, or in your group, make a list of things that people share a need for. You may do this on a sheet of paper or on this page.

Use the list below to get you going. You may include your own ideas, or use the topics below, should they be true for all of you in the group.

- The most important things we have learnt during these sessions were ...
- When we have free time, we enjoy ...
- Important things in our lives are ...
- What parents should do for their children ...

Once your group has completed the list, draw a logo that stands for the things that are true for all of you.

7 Action plan

When I think of myself, the kind of person I want to be and the things I want to be known for, I realize there are:

- some things I need to start doing
- some things I need to do more of
- some things I am happy about and need to keep on doing.

Make ticks in the appropriate columns on the right.

	Start doing …	Do more of …	Keep on doing …
1 Appreciate what is special about myself.	☐	☐	☐
2 Notice what is special about others.	☐	☐	☐
3 Be proud of my culture.	☐	☐	☐
4 Tell my family what I like about them.	☐	☐	☐
5 Love my parents/carers.	☐	☐	☐
6 Thank teachers for their efforts and caring.	☐	☐	☐
7 Make sure that I show interest in others.	☐	☐	☐
8 Make a point of accommodating people with disabilities.	☐	☐	☐
9 Take notice of and assist less fortunate people.	☐	☐	☐
10 Make sure that I am a good family member.	☐	☐	☐
11 Tell others what I appreciate about them.	☐	☐	☐

My time

Failing to plan is like
planning to fail

Outline

Outcomes

The aim of this unit is to offer children helpful tools and strategies for organizing their life by taking control of their time and thinking about their dreams and the things that are important to them.

On completion of this unit, children will be able to:

- understand that time is a resource they have to use with care.

- be aware of how they spend their time.

- list time-wasters.

- name what is important to do.

- prioritize activites.

- plan ahead.

- organize their day.

- think of their future.

- work according to a plan.

- formulate their dreams for the future.

Time is life, it is irreversible and irreplaceable.
To waste your time is to waste your life,
but to master your time is to master your life and make the most of it.

Anonymous

It has been my observation that most people get ahead
during the time that others waste.

Henry Ford

Overview

Like money, time is a valuable resource. But unlike money, it is not renewable. The proper use of time is one of the factors that sets exceptional people apart from the average person. This does not mean that you have to be over organized. It simply means that you know what is important and understand what should be done and when it should be done.

What you dream today may be tomorrow's reality. In his book *The Prophet*, Kahlil Gibran (1955) wrote:

> Yet the time in you is aware of life's timelessness, and knows that yesterday is but today's memory and tomorrow is today's dream.

Failing to plan is like planning to fail

Understanding what you love and where you want to go with your life is a basic requirement in preparing for the future. Starting with the end in mind is particularly relevant in career and life planning. In fact, when children know where they want to go with their lives, school takes on a different meaning.

If you know where you want to be in future, you automatically select suitable opportunities to reach your goals and realize your dreams. Too many young people land in careers that are not best suited to them. They end up being unmotivated, unhappy employees who cannot wait to retire from something that drains them of energy.

However, few people ever seriously think about the future, or plan their lives and inputs around their dreams. Most people know what they don't want, but are not sure of what they truly want.

It is said that 2 per cent of people innovate, create, initiate, activate and make things happen, because they have clear-cut goals. Some 14 per cent of people assist them, observe them or criticize them while they're making it happen. And 84 per cent of people don't know what's going on, except for what the 2 per cent or 14 per cent choose to tell them.

Although most children find it difficult to visualize their future, it is important to start thinking about it. Mastery is the result of talent, opportunities, focused effort, perseverance and refinement of skills. People who start young have an advantage. It does not mean that children should have no time to dream and play, but it does mean that they need to spend some time thinking about themselves – their personalities, their talents and their hopes. When you appreciate yourself, believe in your capabilities and know where you are going, it makes more sense to persevere.

Cooper and Sawaf (1998) have the following to say on this topic:

> A composer can have all the talent of a Mozart and a passionate desire to succeed, but if he believes he cannot compose music, he will come to nothing.

And

> Success requires persistence, the ability not to give up in the face of failure.

Busyness versus productivity

There is the saying that if you want something done, give it to the busy person. Some people simply find a way of getting things done, while others spend their time thinking up excuses while they dawdle their time away.

When you confuse busyness with productivity, you may be very busy all day long without getting the important things done. It helps to have priorities and plan beforehand – even if you have to improvise along the way when things go wrong or unexpected things come up.

Passion + vision + action = success

Being focused is not the same as being obsessed. Despite your dreams and efforts, you have to be flexible in your thinking on your road to the future.

Going with the flow means holding onto your goals lightly (even though they may seem very important) and being willing to change them if something more appropriate comes along. It is that balance between keeping your destination clearly in mind and yet also enjoying the beautiful scenes you encounter along the way, and even being willing to change your destination if life starts taking you in a different direction. In short, it means being firm, yet flexible.

Shakti Gawain (1978)

A positive vision for the future is very powerful. Great leaders throughout history were strong followers of an alluring vision. If you do not have positive expectations of a bright future, what is there to drive you? For many it would be fear – fear of failure, fear of being poor and so on. Thus the 'carrot' versus 'stick' theory (being driven by positive self-motivation versus being driven by fear). Fear could be compared to a force moving you 'away from' something or someone, while a vision creates a force 'towards' a specific goal, which makes it more focused and positively directed.

When you know what you are running from, but you do not know what you want, you do not have a clear goal, and your efforts could be wasted on activities that do not contribute towards your goals. You are, in effect, allowing others or circumstance to direct your life course.

If you are driven by fear, you have higher stress levels and eventually run out of energy. If you are driven by a positive vision of the future, you are energized and life is exciting. This positive mindset helps individuals overcome illness, disappointment and challenges.

Without effort, dreams merely stay dreams. It is when you do what you do with passion and conviction that your actions have direction and meaning. This philosophy of life could be fostered in young people.

Love what you do

Some of us live through time, while others live in time. If you live in time, you are more inclined to be aware of the specific time of the day and will probably be more punctual. Task-driven people seem to be more punctual.

If you live through time, you are probably more interested in people and relationships, and may even at times be late for appointments. This mindset is often linked with the theory of brain dominance suggesting that left-brained people are more punctual and right-brained people are more disorganized. This may be an oversimplification.

In reality, when you are busy with something that you really enjoy and that 'feels like you', you do not mind spending time on it. You may indeed become so involved that time becomes irrelevant to you. Mihaly Csikszentmihalyi (1990) refers to 'being in flow'. It means that you are so comfortable with what you are doing, and it suits your personality so well, that your actions follow almost automatically and effortlessly.

There is no job with inherent meaning. You bestow meaning on your job. Even the simplest of jobs can be satisfying if it is what you want to do. In a workshop for a company, in which employees from different departments and different levels within the organization were represented, a cleaner made the following comment: 'I have realized that I do not want to move up the company ladder. I am happy with what I am doing. Apart from making the building a nicer place to work in, many people come to me and talk to me about their problems. I am in the position to listen to them, and I know that means something to them. That gives my work meaning.'

Meaning is not something you stumble across, like a riddle or the prize to a treasure hunt. Meaning is something you build into your life. You build it out of your own past, out of your affections and loyalties, out of the experience of humankind as it was passed on to you, out of your own talent and understanding, out of the

things you believe in, out of the things for which
you are willing to sacrifice something. The
ingredients are there. You are the only one who
can put them together into that unique pattern
that will be your life. Let it be a life that has
dignity and meaning for you.

Cooper and Sawaf (1998)

Wolfgang Grulke wrote the following inscription to
his daughter in his book *Ten Lessons from the Future*
(2000):

You inspired me to leave a mark on the future.
May you gain the wisdom to choose your ideal
future and thrive in it, happily.

In essence his inscription means that:

- It is often because of the people that we love that
  we aspire to a great future. We want them to be
  proud of us.
- When you choose your future, instead of leaving it
  up to fate or circumstance or other people, you are
  wise.
- To merely hope to survive is not enough. One
  should aim high – to thrive, and be happy.

Resilient learners are learners with high hopes for a
great future. By using this resource book they could
learn to plan their lives and keep on refining their
dreams for the future so that they too might thrive
and be happy one day.

Your life is important.
Honour it.
Fight for your highest possibilities.

Nathaniel Branden (1994)

Guidelines
and
Activity Sheets

Making choices

Learning points

Time, like money is a valuable resource and should be used with care and discretion.

Comments

Go through the rules of the game provided on the activity sheet with the children before they divide into smaller groups. The children are instructed to work in groups of three or four. They select one child who acts as the inheritor and the rest of the group helps to spend the money. The children need to explain to each other what they will do with the money and why they have made their choices. At the end of the activity, learning points should be shared with the larger group. Give positive feedback on wise decisions.

Timing

2 minutes for explaining the rules of the game and forming groups of three or four sitting together

5 minutes discussion time

3 minutes general large group feedback

1 *Making choices*

👥 Small group activity

You have just received £86,400 from an uncle and you have to spend it all wisely!

Rules

1 Everybody in the group has to help you spend the money. You have to agree on what you want to buy and what the price is. The whole group has to agree before you make the final decision.

2 You have five minutes to make your decisions.

3 The money has to be spent before tomorrow evening.

4 Shops will be closed after 5 pm.

5 You have to be at school tomorrow – it is not a school holiday!

6 At the end of the activity, you have to explain to the larger group what you have decided and why you made those choices.

Did you know?
Each of us has 86,400 seconds to spend every day.

Guidelines: Activity Sheet 2

Self-assessment

Learning points

Through unproductive habits we can waste valuable time while we tell ourselves that we plan our time. The reasons could vary – a lack of planning, prioritizing or assertiveness, or by procrastinating or postponing. By identifying your habits or tendencies, we can work on improving our time-management skills.

Comments

Explain to the children that this is a self-assessment and they are going to evaluate themselves with no obligation to give feedback to the group. The aim is to find out where they can improve.

Tip

Ask the children whether they plan their time and whether they know people who do that really well.

Timing

2 minutes explanation

10 minutes for filling in the form and categorizing

5 minutes for discussion and possibly adding to the items on the list, based on personal observations

2 Self-assessment

👤 On your own

Read the statements below and tick the ones that are true for you. You do not need to discuss the results of your self-assessment if you don't feel comfortable to do so.

	A	Tick
1	I know how long it is going to take me to finish a task.	☐
2	Before I do anything, I think about it carefully.	☐
3	I know what I want to be as a grown-up and I have dreams for the future.	☐
	B	
4	I often worry about my schoolwork.	☐
5	I feel I have too much to do.	☐
6	I say yes when someone asks me a favour, even if I am busy.	☐
	C	
7	I am not sure what is important to do.	☐
8	I do not always finish my tasks for the day.	☐
9	I am late for appointments.	☐
	D	
10	I often postpone schoolwork and chores at home.	☐
11	I have long telephone conversations with friends.	☐
12	My room and workspace really needs tidying.	☐

A – Planning for the future

If you have marked all three items, you have a good idea of time and how to plan for the future.

B – Assertiveness (sticking up for yourself)

If you have marked items in this section, you probably need to say 'no' without feeling guilty. You have rights too.

C – Prioritizing (knowing how important tasks are)

If you have marked items in this section, you need to think about what is really important.

D – Postponing

This section is about postponing things till later. If you have marked items in this section, you need to think about your habit of putting things off till later. In the long run, this habit could cause you lots of trouble and you may even miss out on opportunities.

Guidelines: Activity Sheet 3

Using my time

Learning points

By understanding how much time we spend on each activity we can determine whether we need to make adjustments to our activities and lifestyle. This activity sheet gives an indication of whether we have a balance of interests or activities. Later in life this skill becomes crucial when some people turn into workaholics or procrastinators.

Comments

The children have to determine how much time they spend on each activity in a typical day and shade the number of hours from left to right. It can be a good idea to work first in pencil and, only when the children are sure of the number of hours, to then use coloured pencils or felt-tip pens to allocate a colour per category. This will form a colourful graph that will be a visual representation of how time is utilized. If desired, the children could convert the daily figures into a weekly graph (part 2) by multiplying some figures by 7 (resting time for instance), while they multiply work time by 5 and other activities by the number of days they occur. The total amount of time for each activity is then transferred to the weekly graph to determine how the children balance their time.

Before completing part 3, discuss what the children have learnt from doing parts 1 and 2 of the activity. Ask them the following questions:

- How many hours do you spend travelling to school or work?
- What is the average time you spend in front of the TV?
- How much time do you spend talking to family members about important issues like family values, loyalty, difficulty and even everyday issues?
- What do you do that is creative?
- Do you do any community service?

Tip

How to shade the bar chart in part 1:

- Each of the nine activities is given a bar divided into 12 blocks each representing an hour.
- The children colour the sections according to the amount of time they spend on each activity.

Timing

3 minutes explaining the activity

15 minutes for completion

10 minutes for addressing learning points and general discussions

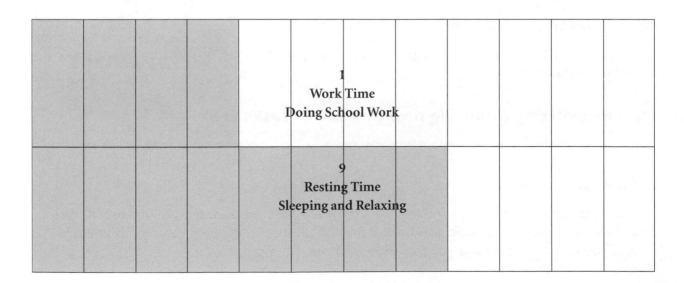

3 Using my time (part 1)

👤 On your own

1 Think about your day. How do you use your time?

2 Use the table below to work out how much time you spend on activities. Each square stands for one hour, so for each hour (or part of an hour) that you spend on the activity, you need to shade one square (or part of it). Fill in the squares from left to right. You may use coloured pens or pencils.

				1 Work Time Doing school work						
				2 Helping Time Helping at home, helping others who need assistance						
				3 Grooming Time Washing and grooming myself, tidying my room						
				4 Serious Play Time Extra curricula activities: team sports, music lessons and so on						
				5 Play Time Being with friends, visiting relatives and having fun						
				6 Best Friend Time Spending time with a special friend						
				7 My Own Time Keeping myself busy with hobbies						
				8 Dream Time Dreaming and thinking						
				9 Resting time Relaxing and sleeping						

👤 Questions to think about

1 What have you learnt about the way in which you spend your time?

2 What should you do more of?

3 Using my time (part 2)

On your own

1 Complete the graph below to determine how much time you spend on the different activities given in part 1 in a **week.**

2 Daily activities such as sleeping should be multiplied by 7 to give your weekly figure.

3 Work time should be multiplied by 5.

4 Extra-curricular time should be multiplied by the number of days you do those activities.

5 Each square stands for ten hours, so for each ten hours (or part of ten hours) that you spend on the activity, you need to shade one square (or part of it). Fill in the squares from bottom to top. You may use coloured pens or pencils.

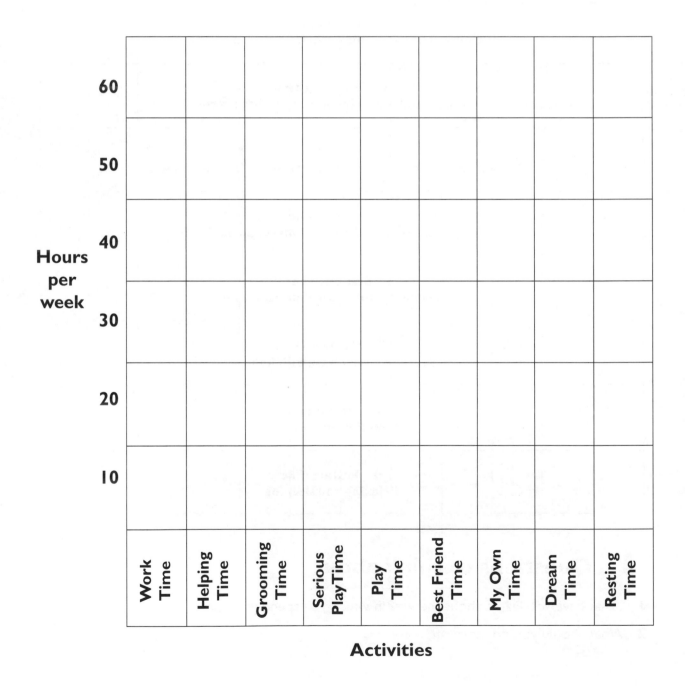

Hours per week

60
50
40
30
20
10

Work Time | Helping Time | Grooming Time | Serious Play Time | Play Time | Best Friend Time | My Own Time | Dream Time | Resting Time

Activities

3 Using my time (part 3)

👤 On your own

Read the following questions and write your answers in the space provided.

1 What have you learnt from doing this activity?

2 What should you do more of?

3 Which activities make you feel more self-confident?

4 How could you spend your time more productively? (Think of activities that make you feel in control of your life and that bring about useful results.)

5 What advice would you give to your friends if they asked you for your opinion on how to use their time?

6 What can you do to ensure that you regularly have good quality time with family or friends? (What is within your control, and how can you convince others to make time for this activity.)

Guidelines: Activity Sheet 4

Time-wasters

Learning points

Time-wasters are things that we do that are not important to us. It may differ from person to person. If we plan our time, we will probably have a better idea of how we really want to spend our day.

Comments

- Ask the children what they consider to be time-wasters and ask them to define 'time-wasters'.
- Discuss the questions with the children and list a few examples of what time-wasters could be.
- Encourage the children to become aware of the time they spend on individual activities.

Tip

Refer to the minutes wasted when a person arrives late, or the time it takes children to settle in before a lesson, and multiply the minutes by the number of periods and the number of days per week or even year. The compound effect is often astounding.

Timing

5 minutes introduction

12 minutes activity

5 minutes general discussion and learning points

4 Time-wasters

♟♟♟♟ Large group discussion

1 Do people who plan their time have less fun?
2 What do you think will happen if you plan your time well?
3 How much time do you spend each day watching TV or playing TV/computer games?
4 How many hours would that be per year?
5 What would be a better way of spending your time?

♟ On your own

Complete the table below by writing down the things that you consider are a waste of time and the amount of time you think is wasted when doing these things.

	Time-wasters	Minutes wasted
1		
2		
3		
4		
5		
6		
7		
8		
	Total amount of time wasted	

♟♟♟♟ Large group discussion

Discuss with the group what you have written in your table.

Guidelines: Activity Sheet 5

Doing what I love

Learning points

When we are involved with something we are interested in, time seems to fly. When we do chores or things we are not interested in, time drags. When we lose our sense of time and become totally absorbed by an activity, we may experience a sense of 'wow!' or of 'being in the flow'. In such cases we are probably doing something we have the talent, interest and skills for.

Imagine doing a job that you enjoy that much! This says something about career choices based on self-knowledge. The right choice will follow easier if we understand ourselves.

Comments

Read through the questions and explain their meaning. The children work in small groups to answer the questions and each child needs to take part. The small groups give feedback to the larger group at the end of the activity.

Tip

As an icebreaker, ask the children to explain to the rest of their small group what their favourite activity or pastime is, and what makes them truly excited.

Timing

3 minutes introduction

12 minutes small group discussion

10 minutes feedback to the larger group

3 minutes conclusion

5 Doing what I love

👥 Small group discussion

Talk to your learning partners in your group and share the following experiences.

1 Think of a time when you were doing something and the time just seemed to fly by.

  a) When did that happen?

  b) What were you doing when that happened?

2 Think of a time when time just dragged on.

  a) When did that happen?

  b) What were you doing when that happened?

3 A 'wow!' moment happens when you are busy with something that you really have a knack for, that truly interests you, and for which you have developed the skills. Think of a time when you did something that worked out absolutely wonderfully and that you found so interesting that you were amazed at what you had accomplished.

  a) When did that happen?

  b) Share the details of the incident with your learning partners.

👥 Large group discussion

What have you learnt from doing this activity? Give feedback to the larger group.

Guidelines: Activity Sheet 6

Prioritizing

Learning points

When we determine what we really need to do, many activities are important. However, when we are not assertive or sure of what we want to achieve, our attention could be distracted by things that do not contribute to our aims.

Comments

- Discuss the meaning of the word 'prioritize'. (Determining how important things are to you.) Discuss what 'activity' means. (Actions or ways of spending time.)
- Talk about the diagram on Activity Sheet 6 and what could potentially fit into each block.
- Encourage small groups to fill in their diagrams and finally check with the large group whether there is agreement on which activities belong to each category.
- Ask the children what they have learnt from doing this activity.

Timing

5 minutes introducing the activity and clarifying the meaning of words

10 minutes of filling in the diagram

5 minutes feedback

2 minutes concluding with learning points

6 Prioritizing

♟♟♟♟ Large group discussion

1 What does it mean to 'prioritize'?

2 What does the word 'activity' mean?

♟♟ Share in pairs

Explain to each other what you think each square in the diagram below stands for and write three activities in each open square.

	Planned activity	Unplanned activity
Important	**A** Activities that you plan beforehand 1 2 3	**B** Things that come up unexpectedly 1 2 3
Not important	**C** Activities that are important to other people 1 2 3	**D** Activities that waste your time 1 2 3

Guidelines: Activity Sheet 7

Planning my day

Learning points

Lists that are put in writing are more helpful than having broad ideas in our head of how we would like to spend our time or what we would like to achieve. Lists order our thoughts and when we can tick-off accomplished tasks, it gives us a sense of achievement while building self-esteem and developing self-discipline. Motivated people are clear on:

- what they want
- why they want it
- how they are going to get it.

Comments

- Briefly explain the meaning of the ratings and offer examples for the list of activities. Activities such as getting dressed, having breakfast, travelling to school and so on can all be on the list, they all need to be done and should therefore be category A activities.
- The children compile their own lists, but can work in pairs or small groups if it seems more productive.
- At the end of the activity, the large group discussion should touch on learning points.

Tip

Ask the children how they think the head of an organization such as a school, company or even a country would function without a diary, priorities and 'to do lists'.

Timing

5 minutes introduction and explaining the lists

10 minutes completing the list and rating activities

5 minutes feedback and sharing important lessons

7 Planning my day

👤 On your own

1 Read through the box below to understand what the ratings A, B, C and D stand for.

2 Using the blank table below, make a list of 10 activities that you will do each week.

3 Mark each task or activity A, B, C or D, depending on how important it is to you.

A Do it now!

You need to do this to make your dreams come true.

B Do tomorrow or the day after tomorrow

These activities are important, but can wait.

C Do within the next week

These activities are not so important.

D Don't do

These activities are just a waste of time. Don't do them!

	Activities	**A/B/C/D**
1		
2		
3		
4		
5		
6		
7		
8		
9		
10		

👤👤👤👤 Large group discussion

What have you learnt from doing this activity? Give feedback to the larger group.

Guidelines: Activity Sheet 8

At the end of the day

Learning points

Resilient people can do self-reflection to assess their inputs and results, learn from experience and develop a healthy, realistic self-concept. Daily self-reflection encourages continuous personal growth and improvement. It also encourages pro-active planning and prioritizing of activities while keeping dreams alive.

Comments

- Ask the children whether they reflect on their daily activities and whether they keep journals to deal with personal issues and keep track of their personal progress.
- Discuss the advantages of doing the 'end of the day test' or 'end of the day thinking'.
- Ask the children to sit back for a moment and think what they will probably be thinking tonight when they do the 'end of the day thinking' activity.

Timing

5 minutes general discussion and reflection

8 At the end of the day

On your own

When you get into bed at night and you put your head on your pillow, ask yourself:

I have just used 24 hours of my life…

am I happy about today?

Yes! ✔

If the answer is yes, say: 'Well done!' to yourself.

No! ✘

If the answer is no, ask yourself what you can do differently tomorrow!

Guidelines: Activity Sheet 9

Steps to success

Learning points

Step-by-step guidelines help to find areas for improvement while assessing current habits and strategies.

Comments

Work through the list with the whole group and ask for inputs and possible additions to the list.

The last part of this activity is for children to integrate the knowledge and insight they have gained so far, and to express it visually through the pictures and verbally when they summarize what they have learnt about time and the use thereof.

- Refer to the third page of the activity sheet. The drawing is a simplified watch.
- Explain to the children that the diagram of the watch is an activity for expressing their personal experience of time.
- The centre part of the watch is for adding drawings, symbols or words to represent activities they want to do and enjoy spending their time on.
- The outer circle of the watch is a space for writing down a saying or quote of their own, which states their appreciation or viewpoint on time; for example, 'Time is like a river', 'Time is money', 'Time is a gift' or anything else they would like to say with regards to time.
- At the end of the activity, each child's completed artwork is to be displayed for the group to appreciate.
- This is also an opportunity for giving positive feedback and expressing appreciation for wisdom, neatness, artwork and so on, especially for those who are not normally in the foreground and need encouragement. Encourage the children to be gracious and acknowledge the work of others.
- Conclude with a general discussion of what they have learnt from doing this activity.

Timing

1 minute introduction

3 minutes reviewing steps to success

5 minutes illustration

5 minutes sharing the meaning of illustrations

1 minute concluding

9 Steps to success (part 1)

If you want to make the most of your time, you could take the following steps.

Step one: decide what is important

- Make a list of what you have to do.

- Mark the important tasks.

- Do the most important things first, even if they are less enjoyable or more difficult.

- Keep to your list – even if you feel like doing something else.

Step two: think smart

- When you have a lot of homework, take a break now and then.

- Keep a jug of water next to you – you need to drink more water when you really need to concentrate.

- Stretch your legs and walk vigorously in between work sessions.

- Take a few deep breaths of fresh air when you have a break.

- Have fruit and nuts for snacks instead of sweets and carbonated cool drinks.

- Make sure you have enough light – not too bright, not too dark.

- Active Baroque music helps your concentrate while you study (classical music that is mostly instrumental and the beat is slightly faster than your heartbeat – well-known composers of this music are Handel, Bach, Vivaldi and Pachelbel). The music puts your brain in an alpha state, which is good for concentration and cuts out distracting sounds.

Step three: know what you want

- Work on your dreams. What do you want for yourself one day?

- How will you know that you have reached your goal?

- Remind yourself of your dreams and goals – put a picture or an object on your table or wall to remind you of your dreams.

9 *Steps to success* (part I continued)

Step four: plan

Have you ever used a wall chart or a table calendar with big squares you can write in? It helps you to see a whole week or month at a time, especially when you need to work on a big assignment or need to finish reading a book.

- Use a diary to plan your week.

- Before you go to bed at night, plan the next day.

- Do your planning in writing.

- Make a list of what you want to do.

- Think carefully about the time it takes you to finish a task. Some tasks take longer than you think. When you plan your day, allow for some 'extra time'.

- Start early – you can only do so much per day.

Step five: just do it!

- When it is time to get up in the morning, just do it. Don't lie in bed a little longer – it messes up your day.

- Finish tasks.

- If an assignment or a task feels too big, break it into smaller parts, such as:
  - › getting the information
  - › finding pictures or illustrations
  - › making a draft
  - › writing the information
  - › tidying the task.

- Don't put things off until later – do it now!

Step six: save time

- Make sure that your table or workspace is neat.

- Learn to say 'no' to unreasonable requests from friends.

- Ask yourself regularly: 'Is this the best use of my time right now?'

- Discuss assignments with classmates while you are at school, it helps to organize your thoughts and you may even get good ideas on how to go about the task.

9 Steps to success (part 2)

👤 On your own

- Use the diagram below to demonstrate your viewpoint on time.

- Use the centre part of the 'watch' to make drawings, symbols or write words that explain how you choose to spend your time. Keep in mind what you want to do, what makes you feel good about the way in which you spend your time, and what you enjoy doing.

- Use the outer circle of the watch to write down a quote or saying about time.

- At the end of the activity, everybody's picture/artwork is going to be part of a display.

- Make a point of finding the best part (something good or nice or useful) in each person's work and compliment them on their work.

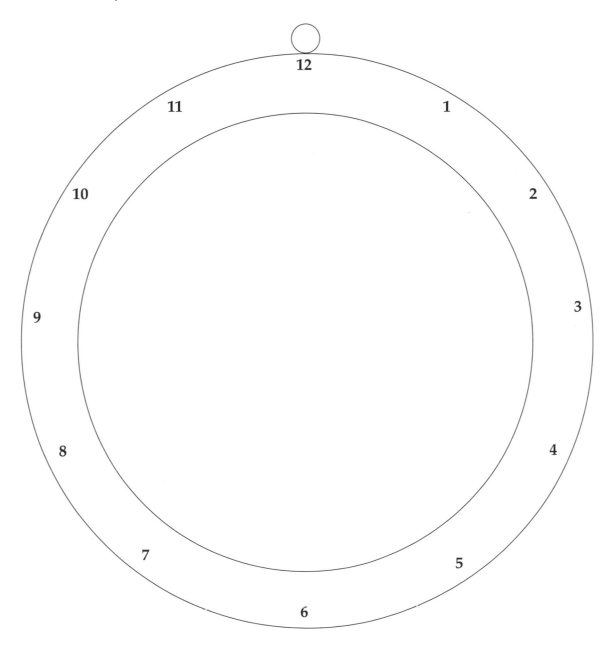

Guidelines: Activity Sheet 10

Time travelling

Learning points

Taking future planning one small step at a time makes the skill less daunting, and is a good starting point for big, long-term dreams. It is not easy to project your thoughts into the future – even as adults we find it difficult.

Comments

Instruct the group to sit in pairs and discuss the steps from the bottom to the top.

Tip

This activity could be done outside if suitable space is available. It is best to do it in pairs, otherwise it might take up too much time. The teacher can play the role of a learning partner in the case of uneven numbers. This should be a high energy activity.

Timing

2 minutes introduction and giving instructions

12 minutes sharing in pairs

5 minutes sharing most interesting dreams in large group

1 minute concluding

10 Time travelling

🏃🏃 Share with a learning partner

1 Find some private space and sit with a learning partner.

2 Share your answers to the questions below.

3 Start at the bottom and work to the top.

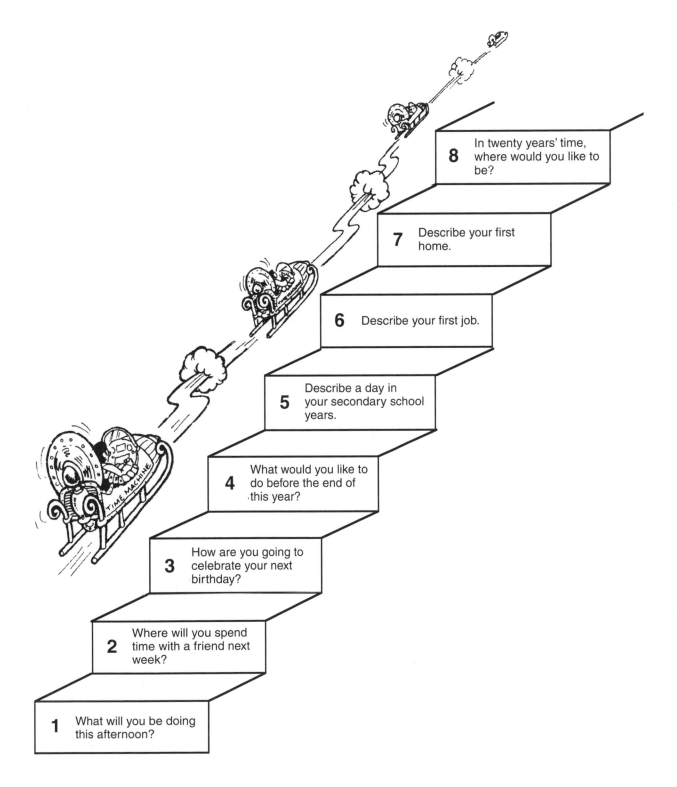

8 In twenty years' time, where would you like to be?

7 Describe your first home.

6 Describe your first job.

5 Describe a day in your secondary school years.

4 What would you like to do before the end of this year?

3 How are you going to celebrate your next birthday?

2 Where will you spend time with a friend next week?

1 What will you be doing this afternoon?

Guidelines: Activity Sheet 11

My dreams

Learning point

It is unrealistic to expect children to know exactly what they want for the future, not even adults find that easy. However, mastery is achieved when we start early in life. Dreams may change, but to create dreams and to refine ideas is an ongoing process. By making a drawing and presenting it to the group, children connect with their dreams more intimately and clarify parts of what they expect from life.

Comments

- Instruct the children to make coloured drawings of their dreams on the activity sheet with the purpose of presenting them to the group.
- The children should be prepared to answer questions about their dreams or to explain what they intended with their drawings.
- Encourage the children to put their drawings up for display in their rooms to remind them of their dreams, to refine their dreams and to keep themselves motivated.

Tip

- This could potentially be a sensitive activity because dreams are very personal. Create a respectful yet light-hearted atmosphere. Refer to mutual respect and trust building as important aspects of being a mature, well-adapted person.
- Explain to the group that this is an individual activity that is only going to be shared with the rest of the group once the drawings are completed. No comments are allowed during the drawing process, and at no time will ridicule or critique of drawings be acceptable.
- This is not an art contest, but rather a form of self-expression.
- Refer to well-known artists and their unique styles.
- Compare this activity to creating graffiti on walls.

Timing

2 minutes instructions

15–20 minutes for drawing

2 minutes per child for presentation to the group

11 *My dreams*

🥄 **On your own**

Make a drawing of your dream for the future. You can use any available medium
– pencil, pens, wax crayons, food colouring and so on. When you have finished,
you are going to share your dream with the rest of the group. You also have to
tell them what makes you think that your dream can come true.

12 Action plan

Because of the things I have learnt doing this unit, I will ...

(tick the items you want to work on)

Action		Tick
1	Think about my dreams for the future.	☐
2	Reflect on my day and learn from it.	☐
3	Remind myself of my dreams.	☐
4	Make lists of what I want to do.	☐
5	Work according to my lists.	☐
6	Be aware of how long it takes me to finish tasks.	☐
7	Decide what is important to me.	☐
8	Plan my day ahead.	☐
9	Learn to say 'no' when people have unreasonable requests.	☐
10	Do things now, without postponing tasks.	☐
11	Finish what I begin.	☐
12	Be careful not to waste time at the expense of more important things.	☐
13	Make sure to fill my day with many worthwhile things.	☐
14	Spend time on things that I enjoy.	☐

Glossary

Acceptance	To keep on fighting and debating things you cannot change simply depletes your personal resources and can alienate you from others. Acceptance brings inner peace and allows you to focus on important issues.
Accountability	To stand forth and be counted
Achievement	Attaining or earning a goal
Acknowledge	Admit that you have something to do with the situation; indicate that you notice
Adapt	To change in order to adjust to new circumstances
Adversity	Bad luck, hardship
Affirmations	Confirmation of the truth of something; a positive reinforcement of a good attribute
Aggressive people	People who force others to comply with their personal rights, desires, feelings and beliefs, at the cost of the others
Alexthymia	Emotional numbness – not feeling at all
Analytical thinking	Taking apart the elements of a situation and evaluating your effect on the situation
Apologizing	Asking forgiveness or expressing regret
Assertive people	People who stand up for their rights, needs, desires and beliefs
Assertiveness	Calmly and consistently standing up for my rights, without losing my temper or giving up my rights
Avoidance	When a person cannot face a situation effectively or does not have the skills to resolve the conflict situation successfully
Behaviour	A way of acting or responding
Blaming	It is your fault! Making others responsible for my situation.
Body language	Information given by posture or motion as opposed to words
Budget	A plan according to which you make, use and save money
Busyness	Keeping oneself busy without necessarily being productive
Cognitive	A process that involves thinking and reasoning
Collaborating	Working through tough feelings to find a mutually satisfying solution for a problem
Commitment	To bind oneself to a cause or promise

Competencies	Abilities or skills
Compromise	Both sides give up something in order to gain something
Confrontation	Facing conflicting issues or persons
Congruent	Aligned or compatible
Connection and cohesion	Making contact with others and maintaining close, meaningful or trusting relationships
Consensual validation	Mutual agreement; more than one person sees it in the same light
Consensus	A general agreement by everyone; staying with that part of the proposal on which everyone has agreed
Constructive discontent	Being unsatisfied to the point of doing something positive about it
Creative thinking	Thinking out of the box, non-conforming
Criticism	Act of judging or giving an opinion
Cultural awareness	Awareness of other's way of living and doing things
Delaying tactics	Strategies aimed at underplaying or cooling off the situation
Delay of gratification	To wait to satisfy a want; postponing impulsive reactions in order to respond appropriately
Democracy	Majority rules
De-role	By telling others that they can be themselves again and that they can let go of the negative emotions or the roles they have played
Discrimination	Make a distinction; it can also mean that you treat a person differently, or as an inferior
Dreams	Subconscious thoughts usually occurring during sleep; also future visions
Egocentric	Self-centred, selfish and based on personal needs and viewpoints
Emotional competencies	Personal and interpersonal competencies that are important for personal satisfaction, relationships and career advancement and leadership
Emotional intelligence	The ability to identify, name and process emotions and use them as a source of information and to connect and empathize with others
Emotional processing	Process of dealing with emotions with the aim of understanding them and learning useful lessons
Empathy	To identify with the experiences of others
Energy levels	Degree to which a person can actively take part; level of energy available to the person

Equal opportunities	Ground rules, the art of listening, giving respectful feedback, no interrupting, looking for mutually acceptable solutions, keeping to the structure of the process and joint planning
Ethnocentric	Relating to the culture and traditions of a race or tribe
Etiquette	Polite manners, conventional rules of behaviour in polite society
Extroverted	Lively, sociable personality
Fear	Unpleasant feeling caused by impending danger or pain
Financial freedom	To be in control of your finances and provide for events unforeseen and the future in general
Flow	Being joyfully absorbed in a task or process that you are so comfortable with, interested in, and capable of doing, that you momentarily lose your sense of time passing; you experience the process as spontaneous and almost effortless
Forgiveness	Very powerful emotional skill, and is particularly relevant in mental health; highly resilient people do not bear grudges
Frame of reference	Viewpoint based on a person's experience, upbringing and belief system
Goals	Aims of someone's ambition
Group conformity	To be part of a group with specific norms and values
Habits	Settled inclination or trend of mind; patterns of behaviour
Impulse control	Resisting the temptation to act immediately
Inquisitive mindset	A tendency to question situations and things
Interdependent	Groups or individuals depending on each other
Internal locus of control	Controlling and motivating yourself as opposed to being controlled by others or circumstances
Intrapersonal skills	The skills of understanding and managing oneself
Intrapreneurship	As employee you take responsibility for the productivity and financial viability of a particular department, which functions as a profit centre
Introverted	The tendency to be shy or quiet or to keep to oneself
Invincible	People who function well despite adversity
Job specific	Related to work content, and to a specific job
Learning point	A fact or the focus of the learning exercise
Life balance	To balance different aspects of one's life

Logical thinking	Reasoning, analysing and thinking in sequence or in an organized manner
Mastery	To reach a very high level of competency – to be very good at it
Meaning	Having significance or deeper spiritual value
Metaphors	A comparison or figure of speech
Name-calling	Lazy-bones! Liar! Thief! Attaching certain attributes to others
Negative emotions	Feelings of discomfort, disapproval, rejection and alienation
Negotiation	Creates opportunities for both sides to win; the objective of negotiation is to resolve the conflict with a mutually satisfying agreement
Non-assertive people	Fail to express their feelings, thoughts and beliefs and act submissively
Optimism	To be confident and inclined to cheerfulness and a positive outlook
Ownership	To take personal responsibility for something
Paradoxical traits	Contradicting or opposing mannerisms, habits or personality characteristics
Paraphrasing	Putting or reformulating another person's statements or remarks in your own words to check for understanding
Personal empowerment	Being confident, informed and equipped to deal with a variety of issues
Personal identity	Being sure of who you are and what you stand for
Personal value system	Set of beliefs and values that guides the emotions and actions of the individual
Polycentric	Centred around other people and their needs as opposed to being self-centred
Potency	Strength or power of influence
Power play	The misuse of power to put another person at a disadvantage for your own benefit; it involves either using forceful tactics to make someone submit to your demands or withholding something another person wants or needs and thereby disempowering the other person – you could use your position of status, privileged information, or physical force
Prejudice	Adverse judgements or opinions formed without factual verification, based on assumptions
Prioritizing	Arranging issues or tasks according to their importance
Private space	Enough space to work in, apart from each other, so that individuals sit on their own, without interference from others

Pro-activity	Anticipating future trends and making provision for them; preparing in advance
Procrastinating	Putting things off until later; delaying action
Productivity	To create, invent, and produce on time
Punctual	To be on time, to do things according to plan
Racism	The belief that human races have distinctive characteristics that make some races superior and so have the right to rule over other races
Resilience	Successful adaptation to risk and adversity and life in general to live a fulfilling, happy life
Resourceful	Having a good, full 'toolkit' of techniques and adapting and responding to circumstances
Respect	Show politeness, kindness and positive regard
Responsible	To have a personal duty towards; to be personally accountable for
Self-acceptance	To appreciate myself and I am committed to myself as I am
Self-actualization	Experiencing life fully, vividly, selflessly, with full concentration and total absorption to become the best you can be
Self-appreciation	To appreciate and value yourself
Self-assessment	Looking at oneself critically to make a judgement
Self-concept	The idea one has of oneself as a person – physically and mentally
Self-confidence	Belief in my ability to deal with life
Self-disclosure	Sharing information about oneself with others
Self-esteem	My rating of myself
Self-knowledge	Understanding myself – my personality, talents and shortcomings
Self-management	Taking control of myself, my time, my emotions and my actions
Self-motivation	Encouraging myself to move forward
Self-reflection	Thinking about oneself and analysing oneself
Self-respect	Appreciating, valuing and feeling positive about myself
Self-responsibility	Taking responsibility for my life and my actions
Self-sufficiency	Being confident about my ability to handle my life, my challenges and to be able to fulfil my needs

Sexism	The assumption that one sex is superior, and therefore has the right to define the other sex's role in society
Solitude	Loneliness and seclusion; being on one's own
Stereotypes	A way of categorizing people – for example of a certain gender, race, religion or career – as being exactly the same
Strokes	Acknowledging something about another person, and giving feedback to that person; strokes can be negative or positive – negative strokes are criticism, positive strokes are compliments
Submissive	Shy, undemanding
Suppress	To overpower
Synergy	To act together in a mutually beneficial way – the end result is more than the sum of the inputs
Tabula rasa	Empty or blank slates – like a clean page, ready to be written on
Time-wasters	Activities that are unproductive
Transferable or functional skills	Skills needed in most work situations, normally taught at school, and include reading, writing and arithmetic
Vision	Foresight – a dream of the future
WIN message	W stands for When, and describes a specific behaviour or action; I stands for 'I' messages and explains how the sender feels; N stands for the negative result of the behaviour

Bibliography

Adair, John (1997) *Effective Communication*, London: Macmillan

Alder, Harry (1999) *The Right Brain Manager*, London: Judy Piatkus (Publishers)

Anderson, Nancy (1994) *Work with Passion: How to Do What You Love for a Living*, Novato, CA: New World Library

Anderson, Walter (1997) *The Confidence Course: Seven Steps to Self-Fulfillment*, New York: HarperCollins

Applewhite, Ashton (1995) *Thinking Positive: Words of Inspiration, Encouragement and Validation for People with AIDS and Those Who Care for Them*, London: Simon & Schuster

Barker, Larry L. and Gaut, Deborah A. (1996) *Communication*, New York: Simon & Schuster

Bays, Brandon (1999) *The Journey*, London: Thorsons

Bernard, B. (1992) 'Peer programs: a major strategy for fostering resilience in kids', *The Peer Facilitator Quarterly*, 9, 3

Blanchard, Ken and Johnson, Spencer (2004) *The One Minute Manager*, London: HarperCollins Busines

Borysenko, Joan and Borysenko, Moroslav (1994) *The Power of the Mind to Heal*, Carlsbad, CA: Hay House

Bovée Courtland, L. and Thill, John V. (1992) *Business Communication Today* Third Edition, New York: McGraw-Hill

Branden, Nathaniel (1994) *The Six Pillars of Self-Esteem*, New York: Bantam Books

Brown, Joseph (1982) *The Spiritual Legacy of the American Indian*, New York: Crossroad Publishing

Burns, Robert (1988) *Coping with Stress*, Cape Town: Maskew Miller Longman

Canfield, Jack and Hansen, Mark Victor (eds) (2000) *Chicken Soup for the Soul*, London: Vermilion

Carlson, Richard (1999) *Don't Sweat the Small Stuff Workbook*, London: Hodder & Stoughton

Cava, Roberta (1990) *Dealing with Difficult People*, London: Judy Piatkus (Publishers)

Chopra, Deepak (1996) *Creating Health*, London: Thorsons

Cohen, Bernice (1999) *Financial Freedom*, London: Orion Business Books

Cooper, Robert and Sawaf, Ayman (1998) *Emotional Intelligence in Business: Executive EQ*, London: Orion Business Books

Cousins, Norman (1979) *Anatomy of an Illness as Perceived by the Patient: Reflections on Healing and Regeneration*, New York,: Bantam

Covey, Stephen R. (1994) *The Seven Habits of Highly Effective People*, London: Simon & Schuster

Covey, Stephen R. (1997) *The Seven Habits of Highly Effective Families*, London: Simon & Schuster

Crane, Thomas G. (2000) *The Heart of Coaching*, San Francisco, CA: FTA Press

Crum, Thomas (1987) *The Magic of Conflict*, London: Simon & Schuster

Csikszentmihalyi, Mihaly (1990) *Flow: The Psychology of Optimal Experience*, London: HarperCollins

De Bono, Edward (1985) *Conflicts: A Better Way to Resolve Them*, London: Penguin

Dobson, James C. (1998) *Solid Answers: America's Foremost Family Counselor Responds to Tough Questions Facing Today's Families*, Wheaton, IL: Tynedale House

Dryden, Gordon and Vos, Jeannette (1994) *The Learning Revolution – The life-long learning programme for the world's finest computer, your amazing brain*, Aylesbury, Bucks: Accelerated Learning Systems

Dyer, Wayne W. (1976) *Your Erroneous Zones*, London: Warner Books

Edmonds, R. (1986) 'Characteristics of effective schools', in U. Neisser (ed.) *The School Achievement of Minority Children: New Perspectives*, Hillsdale, NJ: Lawrence Erlbaum

Fourie, Louis and Codrington, Graeme with Grant-Marshall, Sue (2002) *Mind Over Money*, Parklands, South Africa: Penguin Books

Friedman, M. and Rosenbaum, R. H. (1974) *Type A Behaviour and Your Heart*, New York: Fawcet Crest

Fromm, Erich (1956) *The Art of Loving*, London: HarperCollins

Gardner, Howard (1983) *Frames of Mind*, New York: Basic Books

Garmezy, N. (1985) 'Stress-resistant children: the search for protective factors', in J. E. Stevenson (ed.) *Recent Research in Developmental Psychopathology*, Oxford: Pergamon Press

Garmezy, N. and Rutter, M. (eds) (1983) *Stress, Coping, and Development in Children*, New York: McGraw-Hill

Gawain, Shakti (1978) *Creative Visualization*, Novato, CQ: New World Library

Gawain, Shakti (1997) *The Four Levels of Healing: A Guide to Balancing the Spiritual, Mental, Emotional, and Physical Aspects of Life*, Mill Valley, CA: Narataj Publishing

Gibran, Kahlil (1955) *The Prophet*, Kingswood, Surrey: Windmill Press

Goleman, Daniel (1998) *Working with Emotional Intelligence*, London: Bloomsbury

Gray, John (1999) *How to Get What You Want and Want What You Have*, London: Random House

Gray, John (2002) *What You Feel You Can Heal*, Heart Publishing

Grovè, Shani (1996) *Thank You, Brain*, Cape Town, South Africa: Human & Rousseau

Grovè, Shani (2003) *Think Light*, Pretoria, South Africa: Litera Publications

Grulke, Wolfgang with Silber, Gus (2000) *Ten Lessons from the Future*, Parklands, Souith Africa: @One Communications

Hanks, Kurt (1991) *Motivating People: How to Motivate Others to do What You Want, and Thank You for the Opportunity*, Menlo Park, CA: Crisp Publications

Heystek, Magnus (1995) *World of Money: Don't Say You haven't been Warned!*, South Africa: Cream Publishers

His Holiness the Dalai Lama (2001) *The Art of Living: A Guide to Contentment*, Joy and Fulfillment, London: Thorsons

Holt, John (1994) *How Children Fail*, London: Pitman

Honig, Leonie (1996) *How to Raise Emotionally Intelligent Children*, South Africa: Smile Education

Humphreys, Tony (1996) *The Family – Love it and Leave it*, Dublin: Colourbooks

IBM (1994) *Working Smarter: The Learner Within*, IBM Corporation E.I.S.C.

Jawarski, Joseph (1996) *Synchronicity: The Inner Path of Leadership*, San Francisco: Berrett-Koehler

Kehoe, John (1994) *A Vision of Power and Glory*, West Vancouver, British Columbia: Zoetic

Kinder, Herbert, S. (1993) *Managing the Technical Professional*, Menlo Park, CA: Crisp Publications

Kiyosaki, Robert T. with Lechter, Sharon (1998) *Rich Dad, Poor Dad*, New York: Warner Books

Knight, Sue (1995) *Neuro Linguistic Programming at Work*, London: Nicholas Brealey Publishing

Kübler Ross, Elizabeth (1997) *On Death and Dying*, New York: Touchstone

Luft, Joseph (1963) *Group Processes: An Introduction to Group Dynamics*, Mayfield Publishing Company. Reprinted (1994) in *Experiential Learning Activities: Individual Development*, NY: Pfeiffer & Company

Manning, Matthew (2002) *The Healing Journey*, London: Judy Piatkus (Publishers)

Maslow, Abraham H. (1954) *Motivation and Personality*, New York: Harper and Row

Masuda, M. and Holmes, T. (1978) 'Life events: perceptions and frequencies', *Psychosomatic Medicine*, 40, 3, 236–61

McArdle, Geri E. H. (1995) *Managing Differences*, Menlo Park, CA: Crisp Publications

McWilliams, J. and Roger, John (1990) *You Can't Afford the Luxury of a Negative Thought – A book for people with any life-treatening illness including life*, London: Thorson

Millman, Dan (1998) *The Twelve Gateways to Human Potential*, London: Hodder & Stoughton

Mindpower (1994) *Explore Your Inner Self*, London: Timelife Books, Dorling Kindersley

Mindpower (1995) *Dare to be Yourself*, London: Timelife Books, Dorling Kindersley

Mindpower (1996a) *Develop Your Positive Energies*, London: Timelife Books, Dorling Kindersley

Mindpower (1996b) *Take Control of Your Life*, London: Timelife Books, Dorling Kindersley

Moore, Thomas (1992) *Care of the Soul*, New York: HarperCollins

Orman, Suze (1999) *The Courage to Be Rich*, New York: Riverhead Books

Peck, M. Scott (1978) *The Road Less Travelled*, London: Simon & Schuster

Perls, Thomas T. and Hutter Silver, Margery (1999) *Living to be 100*, New York: Basic Books

Pert, Candace B. (1997) *Molecules of Emotion*, London: Simon & Schuster

Peters, Thomas and Waterman, Robert (1982) *In Search of Excellence*, New York: Harper and Row

Phillips, Maya (1997) *Emotional Excellence: A Course in Self-Mastery*, New York: Element Books

Pienaar, W. and Spoelstra, M. (1992) *Negotiation: Theories, Strategies and Skills*, Cape Town: Juta Academic

Pikes, T., Burrell, B. and Holliday, C. (1998) 'Using academic strategies to build resilience', *Reaching Today's Youth*, 2, 3, 44–7

Radke-Yarrow, M. and Brown, E. (1993) 'Resilience and vulnerability in children of multiple-risk families', *Development and Psychopathology*, 5, 581–92

Reich, Robert (1991) *The Work of Nations*, New York: Alfred Knopf

Rifkin, J. (1995) *The End of Work: The decline of the global labor force and the dawn of the post market era*, New York: Jeremy Tarcher

Robbins, Anthony (1992) *Awaken the Giant Within: How to Take Immediate Control of Your Mental, Emotional, Physical and Financial Destiny*, London: Simon & Schuster

Robert, M. (1982) *Managing Conflict From The Inside Out*, New York: Pfeiffer

Rooth, Edna (1995) *Lifeskills: A Resource Book for Facilitators*, Manzini, Swaziland: Macmillan Boleswa Publishers

Ruiz, Don Miguel (1952) *The Four Agreements: Practical Guide to Personal Freedom*, San Rafael, CA: Amber-Allen Publications

Ruskan, John (1998) *Emotional Clearing*, London: Rider Books (Random House)

Rutter, M. (1987) 'Psychosocial resilience and protective mechanisms', *American Journal of Orthopsychiatry*, 57, 3

Ryback, David (1998) *Putting Emotional Intelligence to Work: Successful leadership is more than IQ*, Boston: Butterworth Heinemann

Schrank, Louise Welsh (1991) *How to Choose the Right Career*, Lincoln Wood, IL: VGM Career Horizon

Seligman, Martin E.P. (1990) *Learned Optimism: How to Change Your Mind and Your Life*, New York: Pocket Books

Senge, Peter M. (1992) *The Fifth Discipline: The Art and Practice of the Learning Organisation*, New York: Doubleday

Siebert, Al (1996) *The Survivor Personality*, New York: Perigee Books (Berkley)

Siegel, Bernie (1990) *Peace, Love and Healing*, London: Rider Books

Smith, Jane (1997) *How to be a better ... Time Manager*, London: Kogan Page

Smith, Manual J. (1975) *When I Say No, I Feel Guilty*, London: Bantam Double Day Publishing

Smith Wasmer, Linda (1997) *Focus of Mind and Body*, New York: Henry Holt

Steiner, Claude with Perry, Paul (1997) *Achieving Emotional Literacy*, London: Bloomsbury

Temoshok, L. and Dreher, H. (1992) *The Type C Connection: The Mind–Body Link to Cancer and Your Health*, New York: Plume

Vaillant, George (1993) *The Wisdom of the Ego*, Cambridge, MA: Harvard University Press

Volpe, Renate (2000) *The Entrepreneurial Mindshift*, Goodwood: Print 24

White, Randall P., Hodgson, Philip and Crainer, Stuart (1996) *The Future of Leadership*, London: Pitman

Wilks, Frances (1998) *Intelligent Emotion*, London: Heinemann

Wismer, Jack N. (1994) *A Communication-Skills Practice*, San Diego, CA: Pfeiffer and Company

Yogananda, Paramahansa (1994) *Sayings of Paramahansa Yogananda, 4th edition*, Los Angeles: Self-Realization Fellowship

Appendix: The National Curriculum – alignment with PSHE and Citizenship

The following table aligns PSHE (Personal, Social and Health Education) and Citizenship outcomes with *The Resilience Series* learning material.

Developing confidence and responsibility and making the most of their abilities		
PSHE and Citizenship outcomes	**The Resilience Series**	
Children should be taught:	Unit	Activity Sheet
a) to talk and write about their opinions and to explain their views on issues that affect themselves and society.	My world (Personal Skills) Diversity (Social Skills)	3 1, 5, 6
b) to recognize their worth as individuals by identifying positive things about themselves and their achievements, seeing their mistakes, making amends and setting personal goals.	Resilience (Personal Skills) Marvellous me (Personal Skills) My time (Personal Skills)	1, 2, 3, 4, 7, 8, 9, 10 1, 2, 3, 7, 8 2, 3, 4, 5, 6, 7, 8, 9, 10, 11, 12
c) to face new challenges positively by collecting information, looking for help, making responsible choices and taking action.	Finding solutions (Social Skills) Moving on (Social Skills)	1, 2, 3, 4, 5, 6, 7, 8, 9, 10, 11 1, 2, 3, 4, 5, 6, 7, 8, 9, 10
d) about the range of jobs carried out by people they know and to understand how they can develop skills to make their own contribution to the future.	Money matters (Social Skills)	1, 11
e) to look after their money and realize that future wants and needs may be met through saving.	Money matters (Social Skills)	1, 2, 3, 4, 5, 6, 7, 8, 9, 10, 12

Preparing to play an active role as citizens		
PSHE and Citizenship outcomes	**The Resilience Series**	
Children should be taught:	Unit	Activity Sheet
a) to research, discuss and debate topical issues, problems and events.	Diversity (Social Skills)	1, 2, 5
b) why and how rules and laws are made and enforced, why different rules are needed in different situations and how to take part in making and changing rules	Diversity (Social Skills)	5
c) to realize the consequences of antisocial behaviours, such as bullying and racism, on individuals and communities.	Emotions (Personal Skills)	5, 7

		Empathy (Social Skills)	4
		Finding solutions	9
d)	that there are different kinds of responsibilities, rights and duties at home, at school and in the community and that these can some time conflict with each other.	My time (Personal Skills)	2, 3, 4, 5, 6, 7
		Finding solutions (Social Skills)	5, 6, 7
e)	to reflect on spiritual, moral, social and cultural issues, using imagination to understand other people's experiences.	My world (Personal Skills)	1, 7
		Diversity (Social Skills)	1, 2, 3, 4, 6, 7
f)	to resolve differences by looking at alternatives, making decisions and explaining choices.	Conflict (Social Skills)	1, 2, 3, 4, 5, 6, 7, 8, 9, 10, 11, 12, 13, 14
g)	what democracy is, and about basic institutions that support it locally and nationally.	Diversity (Social Skills)	5, 6
h)	to recognize the role of voluntary, community and pressure groups.	Diversity (Social Skills)	5
i)	to appreciate the range of national, regional, religious and ethnic identities in the United Kingdom.	My world (Personal Skills)	2, 4, 6
j)	that resources can be allocated in different ways and that these economic choices affect individuals, communities and the sustainability of the environment.	Diversity (Social Skills)	1, 2
k)	to explore how the media present information.	Free to be me (Personal Skills)	1, 2
		Conflict (Social Skills)	8

Developing good relationships and respecting the differences between people		
PSHE and Citizenship outcomes	**The Resilience Series**	
Children should be taught:	**Unit**	**Activity Sheet**
a) to realize that their actions affect themselves and others, to care about other people's feelings and to try to see things from other people's point of view	Emotions (Personal Skills)	1, 2, 3, 4, 5, 6
	Free to be me (Personal Skills)	3, 4, 5, 6, 7, 8, 9, 10, 11
	My world (Personal Skills)	1, 2, 3
	Empathy (Social Skills)	1, 2, 3, 4, 5, 6, 7, 8, 9, 10, 11, 12

		Finding solutions (Social Skills)	5, 6, 10
		Conflict (Social Skills)	6, 7, 8, 9, 10
b)	to think about the lives of people living in other places and times, and people with different values and customs.	Resilience (Personal Skills)	5
		My world (Personal Skills)	1, 2, 3, 4, 5, 6, 7
		Diversity (Social Skills)	1, 2, 3, 4, 5, 6, 7
c)	to be aware of different types of relationship, including marriage and those between friends and families, and to develop the skills to be effective in relationships.	Resilience (Personal Skills)	6, 7, 12
		Marvellous me (Personal Skills)	2, 5
		Emotions (Personal Skills)	6, 7, 8
		Empathy (Social Skills)	3, 4, 6, 7, 8, 9, 10, 11
d)	to realize the nature and consequences of racism, teasing, bullying and aggressive behaviours, and how to respond to them and ask for help	Emotions (Personal Skills)	7, 8
		Finding solutions (Social Skills)	9, 11
e)	to recognize and challenge stereotypes.	My world (Personal Skills)	1, 2, 4, 5, 6, 7
f)	that differences and similarities between people arise from a number of factors, including cultural, ethnic, racial and religious diversity, gender and disability.	My world (Personal Skills)	1, 4, 5, 6, 7
g)	where individuals, families and groups can get help and support.	Finding solutions (Social Skills)	11

Although The *Resilience* Series was designed and developed to comply with/comform to/augment Key Stage 2 PSHE guidelines, both volumes offer learning opportunities for Key Stage 3 and 4 PSHE topics. For example:

Key Stage 4 Outcomes

Developing confidence and responsibility and making the most of their abilities	
Outcome	The Resilience Series
Children should be taught:	Unit
a) to assess their strengths in relation to personality, work and leisure	Resilience (Personal Skills)

	Marvellous me (Personal Skills) My time (Personal Skills)
b) respecting differences between people, developing their own sense of identity	Resilience (Personal Skills) Marvellous me (Personal Skills) My world (Personal Skills) Diversity (Social Skills)
c) recognize how others see them, give and receive constructive feedback	Resilience (Personal Skills) Marvellous me (Personal Skills) My world (Personal Skills) Empathy (Social Skills) Conflict (Social Skills)
d) emotions associated with loss and change caused by death, divorce, separation and new family members	Emotions (Personal Skills) Finding solutions (Social Skills) Moving on (Social Skills)
e) personal qualifications and skills, choices at Key Stage 4, the changing world of work	Money matters (Social Skills)
f) targets for Key Stage 4, seeking out help with career plans	—
g) influences on spending, managing personal money	Money matters (Social Skills)

Developing good relationships and respecting the differences between people	
PSHE and Citizenship outcomes	**The Resilience Series**
Children should be taught:	**Unit**
a) stereotyping, prejudice, bullying, racism and discrimination	My world (Personal Skills) Empathy (Social Skills)

b) empathizing with people different from themselves	My world (Personal Skills) Diversity (Social Skills) Empathy (Social Skills) Free to be me (Personal Skills)
c) the nature of friendship	Free to be me (Personal Skills) Empathy (Social Skills)
d) cultural norms in society, lifestyles and relationships	My world (Personal Skills) Diversity (Social Skills)
e) changes in, and pressure on relationships with friends and family	Finding solutions (Social Skills) Moving on (Social Skills)
f) the role and importance of marriage in family relationships	My world (Personal Skills)
g) the role and feelings of parents and carers, the value of family life	Marvellous me (Personal Skills) Empathy (Social Skills)
h) that goodwill is essential to positive relationships	Empathy (Social Skills) Free to be me (Personal Skills) Conflict (Social Skills)
i) negotiation within relationships, when and how to make compromises	Conflict (Social Skills) Empathy (Social Skills)
j) resisting pressures to do wrong	—
k) communicating confidently with peers and adults	Free to be me (Personal Skills) Conflict (Social Skills)